HALLOWEEN
RECIPES
& CRAFTS

Christine Lyseng Savage
Rosa Poulin
Tamara Eder

Photography by Alan Bibby & Tamara Eder

GHOST
HOUSE

Ghost House Books

The Publisher: Ghost House Books
Distributed by Lone Pine Publishing
10145 – 81 Avenue   1808 – B Street NW, Suite 140
Edmonton, AB, Canada T6E 1W9   Auburn, WA, USA 98001

Website: http://www.ghostbooks.net

National Library of Canada Cataloguing in Publication Data

Savage, Christine Lyseng, 1968–
   Halloween recipes and crafts / Christine Lyseng Savage, Rosa Poulin,
Tamara Eder.

   ISBN 1-894877-10-1

   1. Halloween decorations. 2. Halloween cookery. I. Eder, Tamara,
1974– II. Poulin, Rosa. III. Title.
TT900.H32S28 2003   745.594'1 C2003-911080-X

Editorial Director: Nancy Foulds
Project Editor: Shelagh Kubish
Editorial: Shelagh Kubish, Dawn Loewen
Illustrations Coordinator: Carol Woo
Production Manager: Gene Longson
Book Design, Layout & Production: Elliot Engley
Production Support: Heather Markham, Curtis Pillipow
Cover Design: Curtis Pillipow

Cover Photo: PictureQuest

Photo Credits: All photographs by Alan Bibby or Tamara Eder except Lisa Devlin: page 135; Jen Fafard: page 141; PictureQuest: pages 134, 143, 151, 152.

We acknowledge the financial support of the Government of Canada through the Book Publishing Industry Development Program (BPIDP) for our publishing activities.

PC: *P1*

Contents

Acknowledgments

We heartily thank the many people who were so generous with their time and advice as we completed this book.

Thanks to the Cameron and Janzen families for lending their homes for photo shoots and to La Boheme Restaurant for the space to create, test and photograph the food in the book. Thank you to Carol and Kate for both hospitality and help during the photo shoot. Thanks to Michael Poulin and Tina Mihaljevic for helping with crafts and to Laura Peters and Marg Mearns for advice and encouragement. Thank you to our principal photographer, Alan Bibby, and his assistant Adam Rankin. Jen Fafard provided a lot of guidance and expertise in the early planning stages of this book, for which we thank her.

Introduction

It is a dark, cloudless night—the last night of October. A full yellow moon casts an eerie glow across a row of gray tombstones. In the distance you hear a howling sound. Is it the wind? A coyote? Perhaps neither—it could be a lost and tortured soul, forced to walk the dark earth for all of eternity! This is a night of haunting, of ghouls and ghosts, of grinning jack-o'-lanterns, witches and spooky houses. On this night, you will step out of ordinary existence and into the realm of darkness, nightmare and mischief.

Halloween conjures up all sorts of images—both frightful and fun. For many people, this is the most exciting, spine-chilling night of the year. Children and adults love to transform themselves into unrecognizable creatures for a night of hauntingly good fun. Join the festivities and start preparing for a Halloween celebration that will be the talk of the neighborhood!

Within this book, you will find everything you need to know to prepare for a thrilling, chilling Halloween. Use your imagination and the resources that you have on hand, decorate as much or as little as you wish, and add some simple touches to set the scene for a spooky Halloween. We hope you enjoy trying out the ideas in this book and that they inspire you to celebrate in sinister style!

The History of Halloween

In modern times, we associate Halloween with costumed children going door to door to collect candy and treats. But the beginnings of this annual holiday are a combination of ancient superstitions and the clash of pagan and religious beliefs. Let's look at just why we celebrate this spooky day with twinkling pumpkins, elaborate costumes, trick-or-treating and creepy decorations!

In the oldest civilizations known to us, there have been tales and legends of ghosts, witches, spirits and monsters. These creatures were often associated with darkness and night—a time when things cannot easily be seen. Early people were terrified of the dark, for it represented the unknown and evil. These fears became part of the people's mythologies and were eventually recorded in stories and poems. Darkness still evokes images of frightful creatures, ghosts and mysterious goings-on.

About 2000 years ago, the Celtic people of what is now Ireland, the United Kingdom and northern France held a festival on October 31—their New Year's Eve—to honor Samhain, the god of the dead. This day marked the beginning of harvest and the dark, cold winter, a time often associated with death. Celts believed that at this time, the worlds of the living and the dead came together. They lit huge bonfires to offer sacrifices to their deities and to scare away evil spirits, witches and ghosts, which they believed roamed the earth on this dark night. Because the Celts were afraid of these unknown and mysterious beings, they dressed up in costumes so the spirits wouldn't recognize them. They also put jack-o'-lanterns in their windows to frighten away ghosts and demons.

After the Romans conquered the Celts, religious and secular traditions merged. The Romans called November 1 All Hallows Day, an occasion on which they held a feast to celebrate their saints. The night before became known as All Hallows Evening—which became All Hallows E'en and eventually simply Halloween.

During the latter half of the 19th century, millions of Irish fled the potato famine and immigrated to North America. They, along with other European immigrants, helped to popularize Halloween celebrations on our continent.

Americans began to make Halloween more about community get-togethers and less about spirits and witches. Halloween gradually lost its serious connections with superstition, religion and death and became more focused on parties, games, costumes and festivity. Halloween is now North America's second-largest commercial occasion, and billions of dollars are spent each year on costumes, decorations, parties and treats.

Introduction

Trick-or-treating

The custom of trick-or-treating likely has several origins. The Irish believed that goblins and fairies played pranks on Halloween, so making mischief became part of the festivities. They also used to place bowls of food outside their homes on Halloween night to appease the spirits and prevent them from entering their homes. Another source of this tradition could be the fact that Irish peasants used to go to neighboring houses to collect money and food. A custom from the All Souls' Day parades in England involved poor citizens begging for food and receiving "soul cakes" from families in return for their promise to pray for that family's deceased relatives. This practice was eventually taken over by children who visited the houses in their neighborhood in search of food and money. If homeowners failed to provide treats, they risked being the victims of practical jokes or "tricks."

Halloween colors

In ancient times, black represented night and death, both prominent themes in Halloween tradition. Orange represents autumn and the color of harvest, and it was also the color of the bonfires lit to frighten away ghouls and demons.

Ghosts and skeletons

Because the festival of the Celtic god of the dead, Samhain, was celebrated on October 31, this night has long been associated with images of death and the spirit world.

Witches

People believed that witches flew in on broomsticks to celebrate at a party hosted by the devil and that witches were at the height of their power on Halloween night. It was believed that witches could cast spells on unsuspecting people, transform themselves into different entities and create havoc with black magic.

Black cats

The Celts used to believe that witches sometimes appeared in the form of black cats, so cats were thought to be wicked. Some also believed that cats' bodies played host to the spirits of the dead. A famous superstition is that you will have bad luck if a black cat crosses your path.

Bobbing for apples

The history behind this practice has roots in the Roman worship of Pomona, goddess of the harvest. Apples were thought to be the sacred fruit of the goddess, so they became connected with autumn harvest festivities and Halloween.

Planning a Halloween Party

The moon is full, the sky is darkening and there is a chill in the air. It's October 31—time for the ghoulish ghosts, wicked witches and grim goblins to descend upon your haunted house for the most macabre Halloween party ever!

There are dozens of terrific ideas in this book, but remember not to take on too much or you will end up overwhelmed and too busy to enjoy your own party. It's not necessary to create an elaborate setting or a mile-long buffet. Try a few suggestions from this book, keep things simple and remember that the most important thing is that everyone—including you—has fun. The supplies and equipment that you will need for these easy-to-make crafts, decorations, recipes and costumes—if you don't already have the items in your home—are readily available at craft, department or hardware stores. You can also try toy stores and novelty stores. Improvise and be creative!

Keep the ages of your guests in mind when choosing decorations, activities, recipes and so on. Older children and adults usually love to be frightened, but you need to use caution when younger children are in attendance.

Plan ahead and do as much work in advance as possible. This way, you can sit back and relax once the party starts—and simply enjoy watching as creatures of all kinds descend upon your home on the scariest night of the year!

Invitations

Set the tone for an unforgettable night of thrills and chills by sending out unique and spooky party invitations. Using craft or construction paper in a variety of shades, metallic and colored markers, and decorative touches such as glitter and sequins, you can create original invitations that guests will simply be unable to turn down! Suggestions for designs include black cats, bats, skeletons, ghosts, witches—really, the sky is the limit. Just remember to include all of the essential information: date, time, place and other specifics.

Costumes

Naturally, you'll want to urge your party guests to dress up. There's something about stepping into an alternate identity that simply ensures you will have a wildly good time! Remember to prepare your own costume in advance so that you won't have to worry about that at the last minute. See Creepy Costumes & Menacing Makeup for some excellent suggestions on putting together a frightful costume without investing a lot of time and money.

Setting a spooky scene

Decorating your house and yard for Halloween festivities can be a great deal of fun and it doesn't have to cost a fortune. Get as elaborate as you want, but remember that all you really need in order to have a successful party are willing participants, a few simple props and decorations, spooky music and some munchies!

Have a look at the sections on Outdoor Decorations and Indoor Decorations for a wide variety of terrific decorating ideas. Experiment with lighting to achieve some wonderfully eerie effects. Playing Halloween music (see page 15) is a great way to help set the scene for a night of haunting and fun! Borrow CDs or cassettes of Halloween songs and sound effects from your local library, or purchase your own at music stores. Check out the recipe suggestions in the Devilishly Delectable Treats section—preparing these items is almost as fun as eating them!

Introduction

Party themes

Halloween already being a theme of its own, your party really doesn't require a specific motif. However, if you want to give your decorations and activities some direction, consider some of the following ideas:

Creepy Crawly Critters Bash

Decorate with plastic spiders, bugs and snakes. Drape your house with plenty of fake cobweb. Serve Caterpillar Sandwiches (page 89), Spider Cupcakes (page 94), Gruesome Maggot Cookies (page 95) and Mysterious Bug Punch (page 106).

Pumpkin Carving/ Decorating Party

See the suggestions on page 136 of the Ghoulish Games section. Serve a Jack-o'-Lantern Dip (page 84) and Roasted Pumpkin Seeds (page 69).

Monster Mash

Decorate with a monster theme, set up Dr. Frankenstein's Laboratory (page 137) and serve Beastly Buns (page 86), Eerie Eyeballs (page 82) and drinks with Eyeball Ice Cubes (page 110).

Alien Invasion Party

Decorate with the use of metallic pens, foil and glow-in-the-dark items. Try dressing up as an alien in silver Lycra! Serve foods that are shaped like UFOs—such as crepes, tortillas and cookies—along with Eerie Eyeballs and Glowing Green Cocktails (page 111).

Macabre Movie Party

Show scary movies (see the list on page 15) and play charades using movie titles and phrases. Ensure that movies are age-appropriate.

Scavenger Hunt Party

To keep your guests busy and having a howling good time, organize a scavenger hunt. See the tips on page 145 of the Ghoulish Games section.

Halloween Safety

Ensure that your Halloween party is safe and enjoyable for children and adults alike. The potential dangers are not from the lost souls, witches and ghosts of legend, but rather from candle flames, pumpkin-carving tools, scissors and knives, darkened rooms that limit visibility, car and pedestrian accidents and the like.

You can avoid most potential problems by using good common sense. Here are a few things to keep in mind.

Hosting parties

If you serve treats that contain nuts, advise your guests to ensure that no one (especially children) with nut allergies eats foods that contain nuts.

Use caution with potentially dangerous items such as dry ice, knives, glue guns and candles.

Be a responsible host. Ensure that your adult guests do not consume too much alcohol and that they can get home safely.

Make sure that your house is a safe setting. If you use candles, keep them out of reach and away from areas where they might come in contact with people's costumes. Ensure that hallways are kept clear and that there is good lighting and visibility.

Limit the number of guests and activities as well as the noise level.

Children's parties

Make sure your party is no longer than two or three hours for younger children.

Halloween can be frightening for youngsters, so plan activities carefully.

When children are assisting in creating decorations and costumes, consider using white glue rather than a hot-glue gun. Be cautious with scissors and any potentially harmful items or ingredients.

Preparing for guests

Keep a porch light on so that stairs are easily visible.

Pick up tools, ladders, toys, sprinklers or other objects in the yard so that guests and trick-or-treaters won't trip over them.

Keep your pets away from the front door to avoid frightening children.

Using a flashlight in a jack-o'-lantern is safer than a candle in case the pumpkin is accidentally knocked over, or in case the flame comes in contact with decorations or costumes.

Halloween Music and Scary Movies

Monstrously scary music

These Halloween party songs will get party ghouls dancing:

- "Monster Mash," *Bobby "Boris" Pickett & The Crypt-Kickers*
- "The Purple People Eater," *Sheb Wooley*
- "The Martian Hop," *The Ran-Dells*
- "Attack of the Killer Tomatoes," *Lewis Lee*
- "Werewolves of London," *Warren Zevon*
- "Time Warp," from *The Rocky Horror Picture Show*
- "Thriller," *Michael Jackson*
- "Bad Moon Rising," *CCR*
- "Season of the Witch," *Donovan*

For some spooky background music, try these haunting classics:

- The Funeral March, *Chopin*
- Danse Macabre, *Saint-Saens*
- Tocatta & Fugue in D Minor, *Bach*
- In the Hall of the Mountain King, *Grieg*
- Night on Bald Mountain, *Mussorgsky*

Halloween Spooky Sounds, a CD from Ghost House Books, offers Halloween mood-setting music (ISBN 1-894877-49-7).

Scary movies

For young children:

- It's the Great Pumpkin, Charlie Brown
- Dr. Seuss: It's Grinch Night!
- James and the Giant Peach
- Casper
- The Nightmare Before Christmas
- The Witches

For children ages 12 and up:

- Beetlejuice
- Hocus Pocus
- Dracula
- Frankenstein
- The Uninvited (1944)

For adults:

- The Exorcist
- Halloween series
- Friday the 13th series
- A Scary Movie (and A Scary Movie II)
- Ghostbusters
- Interview with the Vampire
- Practical Magic
- Psycho
- The Amityville Horror
- The Shining
- Carrie
- Sleepy Hollow
- Poltergeist
- Ghosts of Mars
- The Rocky Horror Picture Show
- An American Werewolf in London
- The Day the Earth Stood Still
- The Mummy (and The Mummy Returns)
- Labyrinth
- The Others

Outdoor Decorations

S et a spectacularly sinister scene for a spirited Halloween by making your yard and house look frighteningly haunted—or festive and aglow with light and harvest colors. Whether your front yard is large or small, you can use some of the following ideas to transform it into a frightful display!

If you have a fairly large yard, consider creating a graveyard complete with Terrifying Tombstones, Just-dug Graves and a Rickety Graveyard Fence. Hang some Hovering Ghosts, Hair-raising Bats, Frightful Lanterns or Dangling Skeletons from tree branches. If you live in an apartment or condominium, post Scary Warning Signs, hang some Miniature Floating Ghosts and be sure to display a decorated pumpkin or flickering jack-o'-lantern.

There are many small touches that can help you create a spooky setting. Light up your yard or doorway with clear or orange mini-lights and strategically placed flashlights. Another simple way to enhance the eerie effect is to string artificial cobweb through tree branches, around the entranceway to your house and over your displays and decorations.

PROCEED AT YOUR OWN RISK

Terrifying Tombstones

With the right supplies you can easily set the scene of a ghostly graveyard!

Directions

- Cut Styrofoam sheets into large rectangles of assorted sizes approximately 1–3' (30–90 cm) tall by 1–2' (30–60 cm) wide. Do the cutting outside—it is messy.

Supplies

- ❑ Styrofoam sheets
- ❑ gray acrylic spray paint (see note opposite)
- ❑ black marker with wide tip
- ❑ letter stencils (optional)
- ❑ wooden stakes or wire coat hangers
- ❑ pencil or pen
- ❑ serrated knife or saw
- ❑ paintbrush
- ❑ glue gun (optional)
- ❑ hammer

18

- Using a knife or saw, round off the top corners of some or all of the tombstones to make tombstones of varying sizes.
- Paint each tombstone with gray acrylic paint. Note: paint must be acrylic; ordinary spray paint will make the Styrofoam disintegrate. Let dry.
- With a pen or pencil, sketch out your epitaph and additional designs such as flowers or flourishes.
- Once you have decided on your layout, use a black marker to create an epitaph on each tombstone; use letter stencils if you wish. Use your imagination or try some of the following suggestions:

  ✔ RIP Doug Under   ✔ Here Lies Eliza B. Ware
  ✔ RIP Ima Monster   ✔ Buried Alive
  ✔ Let Me Out!   ✔ Died Too Soon

- Using a glue gun or packing tape, attach tombstones to the wooden stakes. Leave at least 4–6" (10–15 cm) of stake below the tombstones so they can be pushed securely into the ground. Use a hammer to pound the stakes into the ground.
- Alternatively, you can cut two lengths of coat hanger wire approximately 8–12" (20–30 cm) each. Insert one end of each into the base of the tombstone and carefully push the other ends into the grass.

Hints & ideas

- If you have access to a wood-burning tool, use it to burn your designs and epitaphs into the Styrofoam. If you choose to do this, be sure to do your etching before you paint the tombstones.
- Use your imagination and create tombstones with extra detail or interesting shapes added to the top or sides. Cut these from the remaining pieces of Styrofoam and fasten them to tombstones with a glue gun, wire or toothpicks.
- Make small tombstones for a "pet cemetery." Epitaphs might include: Dog Gone, RIP Kitty: 9 Lives Over

Variation

- Instead of using gray paint, use black and silver acrylic spray paints. First, apply the black acrylic paint, paying special attention to fill in any areas that have been etched in. Next, hold the can of silver paint at an angle and give the surface a light, patchy coat to give the headstones the appearance of granite.

Just-dug Graves

These shallow graves give the frightening effect of recently buried bodies. Perhaps the ghouls are about to rise from the dead for a night of Halloween haunting.

Directions

- With scissors, cut the plastic bag so that it is approximately the size of the gravesite or slightly larger. The bag will be underneath the soil, which will make cleaning up much easier.
- With a shovel, place a mound of soil on top of the plastic bag. Pile it up so that it resembles a fresh gravesite.
- Place the shoes or boots or body parts on top of the gravesite at the position where the body's feet would be. You can also place an old pair of gloves where the hands would be.

Hints & ideas

- Consider rigging up flashlights to shine onto the tombstones. These can be discreetly placed within the soil itself or positioned to shine from other areas of your yard.

Supplies

- ☐ large black plastic garbage bag
- ☐ soil
- ☐ pair of old shoes or boots or artificial body parts
- ☐ pair of old gloves (optional)

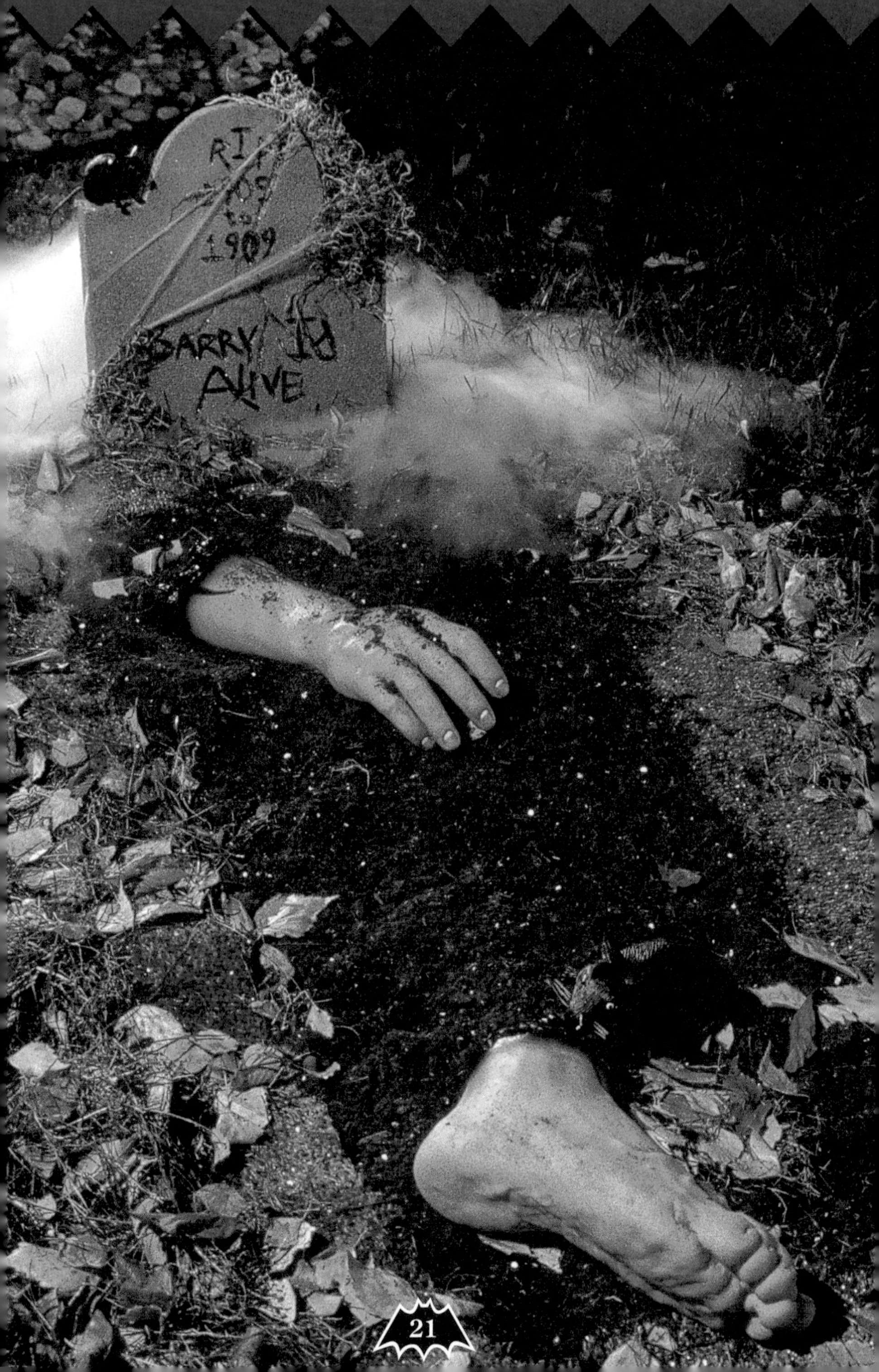
1909
BARRY ALIVE

Rickety Graveyard Fence

A great way to highlight your graveyard and partially enclose the area is to construct a simple picket fence.

Supplies

- wooden stakes, approximately 24" (60 cm) in length
- 1" (2.5 cm) trim boards
- white or light gray exterior paint
- ¾" (2 cm) nails
- paintbrush
- measuring tape
- table saw
- pencil
- hammer

Directions

- Paint the stakes and trim boards with white or gray paint.
- Determine the size of your graveyard. Cut the trim boards to the proper lengths to extend around the graveyard.
- Draw a pencil mark approximately 4–6" (10–15 cm) from the top of each stake.

- Nail the trim boards to the stakes at the pencil marks, spacing the stakes about 12" (30 cm) apart.
- Hammer the stakes into the ground to form a picket fence.

Hints & ideas

- If you want to make your fence appear old and weathered, wear latex gloves and lightly pat on some marks with black and/or green acrylic paint.

Scary Warning Sign

Guests or trick-or-treaters will be wary of proceeding once they catch sight of these sinister warning signs posted along your walkway.

Directions

- Cut the cardboard into the sizes and shapes that you want your signs to be.
- In pencil, sketch a warning message on each sign. This way, you can ensure that your message will fit before you begin to paint.
- Paint the warnings on your signs, using wide letters that are easy to read. Some message ideas are listed below. If you want the words to appear especially creepy, let the paint run down slightly so that the letters appear to be "dripping."
- Glue or tape the signs to the stakes.
- Hammer the stakes into the ground, making sure that they are visible to passersby.

Supplies

- ❑ cardboard
- ❑ paints
- ❑ wooden stakes
- ❑ glue gun or clear packing tape
- ❑ scissors
- ❑ pencil
- ❑ paintbrush
- ❑ hammer

Hints & ideas

- Use some of the messages listed here, or be creative and come up with some of your own.
- ✔ **Proceed at Your Own Risk**
- ✔ **Beware!**
- ✔ **Turn Back!**
- ✔ **Danger: Monsters Ahead**
- ✔ **Haunted House—Do Not Enter!**

Miniature Floating Ghosts

Supplies

- white cotton fabric
- wire mesh, fine
- glue (spray glue works best)
- small craft eyes or black fabric pen
- thread or fishing line
- craft scissors
- needle

Directions

- Cut squares of white fabric (at least 18" × 18" or 46 cm × 46 cm for each ghost).
- Cut the same number of mesh pieces of equal size.
- Coat each mesh square with glue and attach a piece of fabric to it.
- Place the center of each glued square over your fist to form the ghost's head. Form the folds of material outward at the bottom to give the illusion that the ghost is floating.
- Attach a pair of eyes to each ghost's face or draw eyes with a fabric pen.
- With a needle, attach thread or fishing line to the top of each ghost for hanging.

Hints & ideas

- These ghosts are small enough that you can have a couple hanging at your front entry, from trees and shrubs or from planter hangers.
- Miniature Floating Ghosts make great indoor decorations too. Hang them from banisters, chair backs or door frames.

Hovering Ghosts

Create an eerie effect by hanging ghosts of various sizes from tree branches or fence posts.

Supplies

- ❑ round white balloons
- ❑ white plastic garbage bags
- ❑ white string
- ❑ tape
- ❑ black marker
- ❑ fishing line or string
- ❑ scissors
- ❑ large needle

Directions

- Blow up a balloon and tie the end.
- Cover the balloon with a white garbage bag.
- Gather the bag around the bottom of the balloon and, with a piece of string, tie it around the "neck."
- Tape down the corner(s) of the bag that are on top of the ghost's "head."
- Using a black marker, draw a scary face on the ghost.
- With a needle, carefully thread a long piece of fishing line or string through the plastic at the top of the ghost's head. Be sure not to pop the balloon.
- Suspend the ghosts from tree branches or other locations in your yard.

Frightful Lanterns

Transform tin cans into simple lanterns. You can use a variety of sizes of cans and candles for different effects. Line them up on a railing or porch, or hang them from planter hangers in your yard.

Directions

- With a black marker, draw a jack-o'-lantern face, or another design of your choice, on each tin can.
- Fill the cans to within 2" (5 cm) from the top full with water. Freeze until solid.
- Remove tin cans from freezer. While the water is still frozen, use a hammer and nail to punch small holes along the lines of your designs.
- Punch two larger holes at the top of the cans if you plan to hang them.
- Allow the ice to melt. Run hot water over the cans to speed the melting process. Dry the cans completely.
- Lightly coat the cans with orange spray paint. Let dry.
- With a black marker or black paint and a paintbrush, color in the facial features (or portions of other designs that you might create). Allow paint to dry.
- If you intend to hang the cans, use wire or fishing line to create hangers. Bend wire or tie line into the two holes at the top of each can.
- Insert tea lights or other candles and arrange the cans in your yard or entranceway.

Supplies

- ☐ empty tin cans, washed and labels removed
- ☐ black marker
- ☐ orange spray paint
- ☐ black paint (optional)
- ☐ thin wire or fishing line
- ☐ small candles
- ☐ hammer
- ☐ nail
- ☐ paintbrush
- ☐ wire cutter

Hints & ideas

- Do not put lanterns at a level or location where they might be a fire hazard for trick-or-treaters or other visitors. Also, ensure that your handles are not too close to the flame.

27

Hair-raising Bat

There's nothing like bats to give people the heebie-jeebies. Hang a couple of these creepy creatures over your front door or have them appear to be flying around one of your trees.

Supplies
(to make 1 bat)

- ❏ wire clothing hanger
- ❏ wire, 26-gauge
- ❏ 2 black foam sheets, 12" × 18" (30 cm × 46 cm)
- ❏ glow-in-the-dark acrylic paint
- ❏ red acrylic paint
- ❏ scissors
- ❏ glue gun
- ❏ wire cutters
- ❏ fishing line

Directions

- Squeeze the top and bottom of the hanger together on each side. Secure both sides with 26-gauge wire. Straighten the hook of the clothing hanger or cut the hook off with wire cutters.

- Copy the pattern shown opposite, enlarging as necessary. The width of the bat, wing tip to wing tip, should take up the whole 18" (46 cm) width of the foam. Place the pattern on the foam sheet and trace it on. Carefully cut it out. Repeat on the other sheet of foam, to create a front and a back of the bat.

- Place the hanger on top of one side of the bat and cover it with the other piece.

- Using a glue gun, attach the two foam pieces together. (If necessary, bend the hanger to fit between the bat pieces properly.)

- With glow-in-the-dark paint, add scary bat eyes. Accent with red paint.

- Hang the bats with fishing line.

- You can bend the wire in the wings to make it look more as if the bat wings are bent for flying.

Hints & ideas

- You can also use these bats for indoor decorations. Hang them from ceilings or banisters, or place them in bathrooms to frighten guests when they switch on the light.
- Place the fishing twine through the bat slightly off-center, toward the head, so when it hangs, the bat is at an angle as if it is flying up.

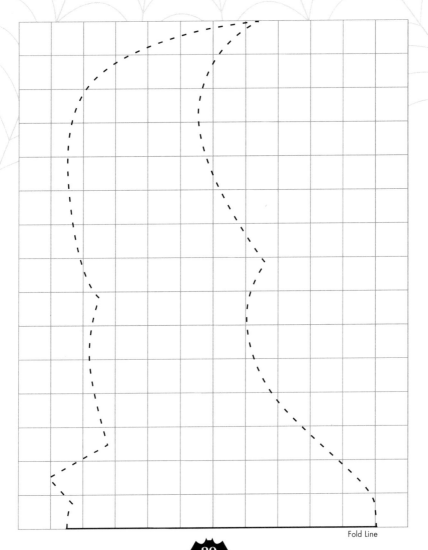

Fold Line

Dangling Skeleton

Give your gallon milk jugs a new afterlife as a spooky skeleton.

Supplies

- eight 1-gallon (4-liter) plastic milk jugs, washed out and dried
- black marker
- scissors
- utility knife
- hole punch
- glue gun
- string or fishing line

Directions

- Use one jug for the head. Using a black marker, fill in the two circular indentations in the jug that are opposite the handle. These will be the skeleton's eyes. Turn the jug upside down and use the black marker to draw on a nose and mouth. Make two small cuts at the top of the jug so you can loop a string through them to hang up the skeleton.

- Use one jug for the torso. Keeping the jug upright, draw a rib cage on the jug. Cut out the rib cage with a utility knife, leaving the ribs intact and cutting around them (see picture for guideline). Use a glue gun to glue this torso to the head at the spouts of each jug.

- Cut the handles off two jugs to use for shoulders, leaving a bit of plastic around each end of the handle. Attach the shoulders to the torso with a glue gun. Use a hole punch to punch a hole at the end of each shoulder section. You will attach the arms to the shoulders using these holes.

- For the hips, use another jug. Cut its bottom off, up to a point 4½" (11 cm) from the bottom. Turn the jug over. Cut the edge of each side of this jug into a wave shape that goes up at the corners (see picture). Punch holes in two opposite sides—this is where the skeleton's legs will be attached. Set aside.

- Create a waist by cutting the spouts from two milk jugs, leaving about ½" (13 mm) plastic on each spout. Use a glue gun to glue these spouts together (one will be turned upside down). After the glue has cooled, glue the waist to the bottom of the torso and the top of the hips.

- Cut eight long bone shapes from the rounded corner sections of three jugs. Punch a hole in both ends of all eight bone pieces. Cut out a center strip from four of these bones; these will be the lower limbs. For each leg, attach two bones together—one that is intact to one that has its center cut out. Attach the leg to the hips by tying a piece of string or fishing line through the holes. Ensure that the bone that is intact is closest to the hips. Repeat the process for each arm, and attach the arms to the shoulders.

- Cut hands and feet out of the side of a jug. Punch holes in the hands and feet and attach them to the arms and legs.

Giant Spider

Arachnophobes of all ages will get a chill when they come across this huge black spider perched menacingly on your driveway or front yard.

Directions

- To form the spider's body, take one garbage bag and stuff it full of newspaper. Twist it closed and secure with a twist tie or tape.
- To form a leg, cut one garbage bag down both long sides at the seams. Open the bag so that it forms a long, large rectangle. Tape the two long ends together to form a long tube. Twist the center of the bag several times to form a joint.
  - Stuff newspaper into the open ends of the leg until it is round and full. Secure both ends with tape or a twist tie.
  - With the remaining three garbage bags, repeat to make three more long tubes.

Supplies

- ❑ 5 large black plastic garbage bags
- ❑ twist ties
- ❑ crumpled newspapers
- ❑ black electrical tape
- ❑ craft foam: yellow, red, black, green
- ❑ tape or glue
- ❑ scissors
- ❑ pencil

- Cut eyes and fangs out of craft foam. Tape or glue the eyes and fangs onto the body of the spider.
- Use black electrical tape to fasten the four legs to the spider's body.
- Position the legs so that they bend at the joints. Display the spider on your lawn or driveway.

Hints & ideas

- Place your spider on a low platform or table to raise it up slightly and make it more prominent and visible.

Menacing Man

Supplies

- ❏ chair, preferably one that looks old and weathered
- ❏ creepy mask, such as a ghoul or monster
- ❏ crumpled newspapers
- ❏ clothes: shirt, pants, gloves, hat, boots
- ❏ safety pins
- ❏ scissors
- ❏ tape

Sit this frightening character near your front doorstep, and your guests and trick-or-treaters will be in for a shocking surprise.

Directions

- Place the chair on the porch or wherever you want to set up the Menacing Man.
- Use newspaper to stuff the mask.
- Stuff the shirt full of newspaper. Ensure that the arms are able to bend. Using a piece of the black garbage bag, cover the newspaper that shows through the neck area of the shirt.
- Stuff the pants with newspaper. Tuck the shirt into the pants and fasten them together with safety pins.
- Fill the gloves with newspaper and insert them into the cuffs of the shirt. Secure with safety pins if necessary.
- Sit the Menacing Man in the chair and position his arms and legs. If necessary, secure the body to the chair by taping it discreetly. Prop the head on the body.
- Secure the stuffed mask to the body with tape or pins.

Hints & ideas

- For a creepy variation, have the man holding his own head in his hands.

Window Decorations

Customize decorations to fit your window; with light shining through the tissue paper at dusk, your windows become a glowing work of art.

Supplies

- ☐ craft paper
- ☐ black construction paper
- ☐ orange or yellow tissue paper
- ☐ scissors
- ☐ clear packing tape

Directions

- Measure the window you will be making the decoration for. Draw a pattern for your window decoration on a piece of craft paper the same size as what you want the final decoration to be. If using our design, enlarge the pattern onto brown paper the same size as the construction paper.

- From the craft paper, create a pattern by cutting out the shapes that you want to remain black in your window decoration. Transfer your pattern to the construction paper. Leaving a border of at least 2" (5 cm) on each side of the window decoration, cut out any designs that you want to be black. In our design (see windows at left of door in photo), the outline of the house, the floating ghosts, the trees and the moon were cut out of the construction paper.
- Add detail and definition by cutting out any features (windows in a building, eyes in a face, a shape on a moon, outline of tombstones) for which you want the tissue paper to shine through. For letters, draw the letters on the construction paper and then cut them out of the construction paper. This is a time-consuming job and must be done carefully, so allow yourself time to work quietly.
- On the back of the construction paper, tape tissue paper, making sure to cover all the holes you cut out.

Outdoor Decorations

Hints & ideas

- It helps to have another person to work with you, as one person can hold the tissue paper smooth and slightly taut while the other person tapes the paper into place.

Variation

- A simpler window treatment can be created using heavy-weight fabric interfacing and brown craft paper (see photo). Create a background and pattern from the craft paper. Cut out a shape from the craft paper. Tape the interfacing to the craft paper. The light will shine through the interfacing.

Halloween Flag

Flag poles that display seasonal flags are very popular these days. Follow our steps so a spooky-looking ghost can come hang around at your house.

Supplies

- ❑ brown craft paper
- ❑ heavy-weight fabric interfacing
- ❑ scissors
- ❑ tape
- ❑ thread
- ❑ sewing machine or needles for hand sewing

Directions

- Draw the shape you desire on a piece of brown craft paper the same size that you'd like the flag to be. To follow our pattern, draw a grid on your craft paper and transfer our pattern to your own grid, square by square.
- Cut the shape out of the craft paper and set aside.
- Cut a piece of interfacing to the size of flag you want. Leave a few inches at the top of the interfacing so that you can create a hem large enough for your flag pole to fit through.
- Tape the pattern onto your piece of interfacing; cut the interfacing, following the pattern.

- Machine or hand sew a hem at the top of the flag, creating an opening large enough so that the flag will easily slip onto the pole.
- Hang up the flag and watch it blow!

Hints & ideas

- Interfacing is a good weight for this craft, as it is crisp yet will still allow your flag to blow in the wind.
- This easy craft can be made more complicated if you wish by using different fabrics and colors.
- Use glow-in-the-dark fabric or draw on accents with a glow-in-the-dark pen.

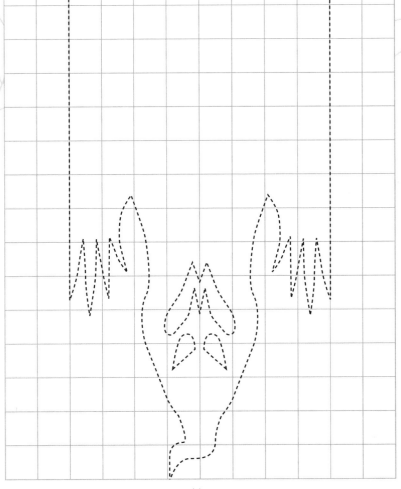

Indoor Decorations

Everyone loves the frightening idea of entering a haunted house—complete with ghosts, witches, goblins and creepy critters! Transform your home into something spooky by creating some of these indoor decorations. Some are easier to assemble than others, but all set the scene for a bone-chilling good time.

As with all of the decorating ideas in this book, these are simply some suggestions. Adapt the decorations depending on personal preference or which supplies you have on hand. Use your imagination and don't feel that you have to spend days and days decorating. A few simple displays or decorations, combined with some eerie music and tasty snacks, are all you need to create a successful haunted house party!

Setting a Spooky Party Scene

- Keep the age group of your guests in mind when choosing your decorations. Some might be too frightening for younger children.
- Purchase paper plates with Halloween designs on them or use black paper plates for a dark and spooky table. Add black napkins and even black or orange plastic cutlery.
- Draw jack-o'-lantern faces on orange plastic placemats.
- Make white napkins into ghosts by tying small ribbons around their "necks" and applying two small black sticker dots for eyes.
- Give your guests the shivers by placing giant plastic rats, which can be purchased at novelty stores or toy stores, on the food table.
- Create an attractive table centerpiece of small pumpkins, decorative gourds, dried cornstalks and dried leaves or flowers. Some of the small craft items in the Party Favors & Crafts section would make terrific decorative touches to add to your buffet or dinner table.

Lighting a Haunted House

Lighting can help you to achieve some frightening effects.

Directions

- Candles provide a lovely flickering light that can be quite spooky. A candle chandelier looks terrific with black, orange or ivory candles. Novelty stores often sell candles shaped like skulls or pumpkins.
- Try using orange or yellow light bulbs to provide rooms with an eerie glow.
- Black lights are great for creating a creepy mood in a small area. Use them with a display of glow-in-the-dark skeletons, bugs, bats and signs. Be cautious, as these bulbs heat up very quickly.
- Hang strings of orange indoor mini-lights from your railings or around a window or door frame.
- Use flashlights as an alternative to candles or to aim beams of light on decorations that you wish to draw attention to. If the beam of light is too bright, try fastening some colored cellophane over the end of the flashlight.

Hints & ideas

- Keep your lighting fairly low, as we all know there is something very scary about darkness. Of course, make sure that your house is lit enough so that it is safe and guests can find their way around!
- Try some of the many decorations and crafts in this book that incorporate candles. These add both light and drama to your party setting.
- Add wax stickers in Halloween designs (e.g., jack-o'-lanterns, bats, spiders, ghosts) to black, orange or white candles.
- Be cautious when using candles, and keep them out of children's reach.
- Instead of inserting colored light bulbs, try draping a thin orange, green or black scarf or piece of fabric over lamps. Ensure that the material is flame resistant.

Cheesecloth Ghosts

Place a couple of these in your foyer or living room or, if you wish to prevent party guests from going upstairs, set them up on the staircase to block the way.

Supplies

For each ghost:

- ☐ 1 bag of cheesecloth
- ☐ 1 large white balloon
- ☐ 1 white plastic garbage bag
- ☐ newspaper
- ☐ black electrical tape, wide
- ☐ iron
- ☐ scissors

Directions

- With an iron on low heat, iron out the wrinkles on the piece of cheesecloth.
- Blow up the balloon and tie the end.
- Insert the balloon into a white garbage bag. This will end up being the head of the ghost.
- Fill the remainder of the bag with crunched-up newspaper. Mold the bag so that it resembles the shape of a ghost's body.
- Drape cheesecloth over the garbage bag. If you have enough cheesecloth, apply two layers.
- Cut a piece of electrical tape into a pair of eyes and attach them to the head of the ghost.

Hints & ideas

- Make a family of ghosts. Be creative!
- For a spooky effect, add scary-looking eyes and drape your ghost display with fake cobwebs and a couple of plastic spiders.

Halloween Paper Chains

Simple paper chains of bats, ghosts and jack-o'-lanterns make spooky decorations.

Directions

- Fold a long sheet of paper back and forth accordion-style, into squares.
- Draw your design, making sure that it extends close to each folded edge and allows for the figures to join across the folds.
  - Carefully cut out the design, ensuring that you leave a portion of the folded sides intact.
    - Gently extend the paper chain.
      - Decorate the paper chains using the following suggestions:
        - **Ghosts** Use a black marker to draw on eyes and a spooky mouth.
          - **Jack-o'-lanterns** Use a black marker to draw jack-o'-lantern faces, or cut out eyes, noses and mouths from black paper and glue on.
            - **Bats** Glue eyes cut from yellow or silver paper onto the bats.
              - Hang the streamers on a wall, along a stair banister or around a table with removable adhesive or thumbtacks.

Supplies

- long sheets of black, white and orange paper, at least 8" (20 cm) wide
- black marker
- paper in contrasting colors (optional)
- removable adhesive or thumbtacks
- pencil or pen
- scissors
- glue

Hovering Bats

A haunted house isn't complete without a few creepy bats hanging around!

Directions

- Enlarge the pattern to the desired size and cut it out.
- Fold the piece of construction paper in half.
- Copy the pattern onto the construction paper by tracing around the outside of it. Ensure that the center of the bat's body is placed directly alongside the fold of the paper.
- Cut out the bat.
- Use a white or yellow marker to give the bat's eyes an eerie color.

Supplies

For each bat:

- ❏ tracing paper
- ❏ black or brown construction paper
- ❏ yellow or white markers
- ❏ piece of black string, approximately 3' (1 m) long
- ❏ thumbtack or small hook
- ❏ pencil
- ❏ scissors

- Cut out small holes at the tops of the bat's wings. Thread the piece of string through each hole and knot on the back of the bat.
- Hang the bat with a thumbtack or a small hook.

Hints & ideas

- To startle unsuspecting visitors, try hanging a Hovering Bat in your guest bathroom.
- Hang bats at eye level in open doorways throughout your house.

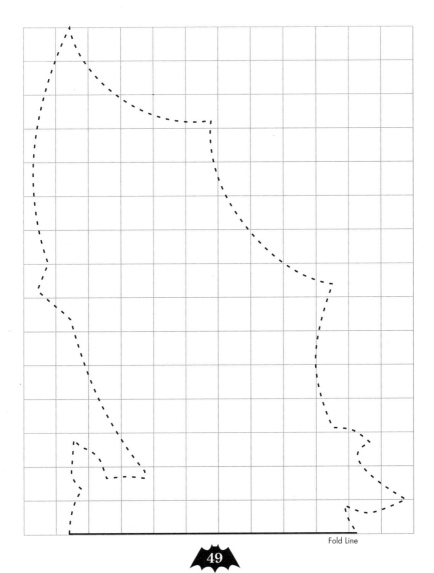

Fold Line

Spooky Candle Centerpiece

These dripping candles evoke images of dark nights in a very haunted house!

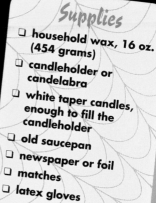

Supplies

- ☐ household wax, 16 oz. (454 grams)
- ☐ candleholder or candelabra
- ☐ white taper candles, enough to fill the candleholder
- ☐ old saucepan
- ☐ newspaper or foil
- ☐ matches
- ☐ latex gloves

Directions

- Melt the wax in the saucepan. Once it has completely melted, let it cool for 15–20 minutes in the pan. Melt just a little wax at a time so that it remains at the right consistency for pouring.
- Insert candles into the candleholder and then set it on some newspaper or foil, which will catch the drips. Light the candles and let them burn for about five minutes, then blow them out.
- Wear latex gloves. Using a tablespoon, slowly drip melted wax at the top of the candle. Do not cover the wick with wax. Continue this process until you are satisfied with the effect. If the melted wax in the saucepan starts to harden, remelt it as necessary.

Hints & ideas

- We were able to purchase a small saucepan for just a few dollars and used that for melting the wax.
- It can be difficult to find a plain candleholder; if you can't find one, use your imagination—the one that we used had apple decorations on it, which we painted to look like orange pumpkins!
- Ensure that you pour the wax very slowly, which allows the drips to form more effectively.

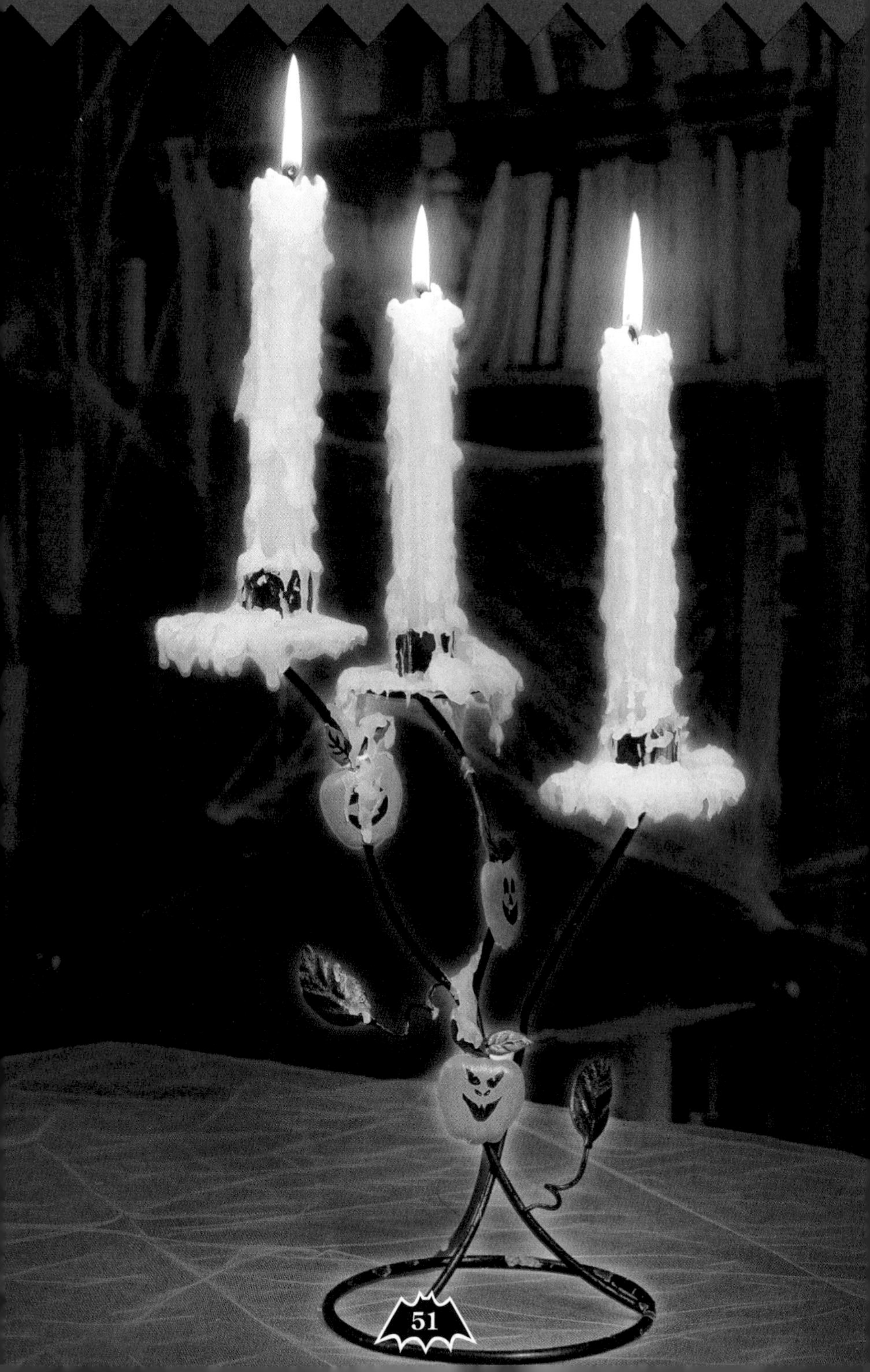

Glowing Candy Corn Pot

Supplies

- ❑ 1 terra-cotta pot, 5–7" (13–18 cm) diameter
- ❑ acrylic paint sealer
- ❑ acrylic paint: yellow, white, orange
- ❑ Styrofoam circle, 1" (2.5 cm) smaller in diameter than pot
- ❑ yellow or orange pillar candle
- ❑ candy corn
- ❑ masking tape
- ❑ paintbrush
- ❑ glue gun

Create a colorful Halloween pot that serves as both candy container and candleholder.

Directions

- Seal the pot with acrylic paint sealer.
- Carefully wrap a piece of masking tape around the pot, approximately 2–2½" (5–6.5 cm) up from the bottom.
- Paint the bottom section of the pot with yellow acrylic paint.
- Paint the rim of the pot with white acrylic paint. Let dry.
- Wrap a piece of masking tape around the pot so that it lines up with the top edge of the yellow painted section.
- Paint the middle section of the pot with orange acrylic paint. Let dry.
- Seal with acrylic paint sealer.
- With a glue gun, apply hot glue around the rim of the Styrofoam circle. Carefully place the Styrofoam circle inside the pot.
- Apply glue to the bottom of candle. Attach it to the center of the piece of Styrofoam.
- Once the glue has dried, fill the pot with candy corn.

Hints & ideas

- For a simpler variation, fill a bowl, jar or small glass vase with candy corn. Set a small glass candleholder in the center of the candy corn and then add more candy around it. Light a tea light candle inside the candleholder for a glowing display of orange and yellow.
- Extinguish the candle before eating the candy corn.

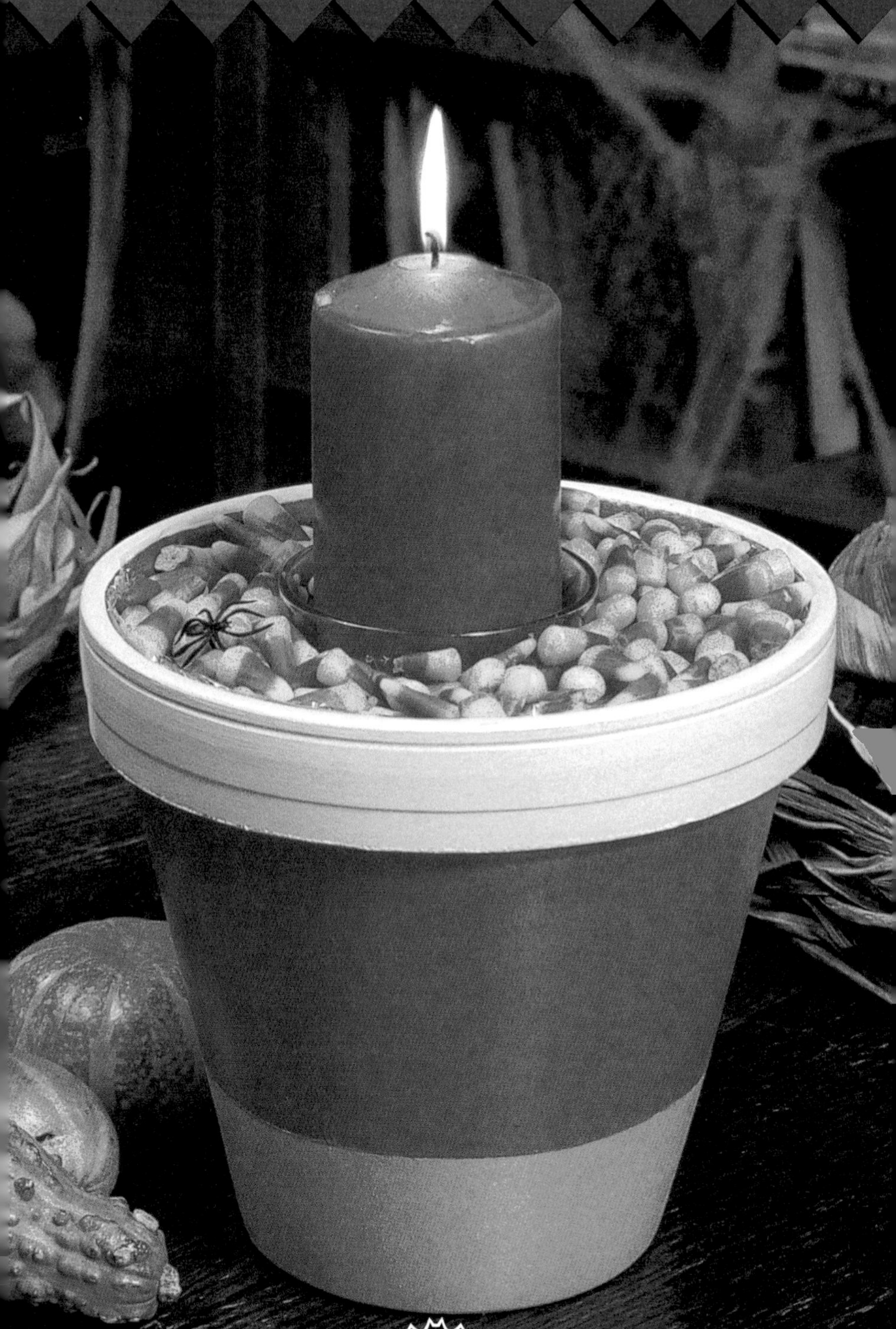

Glowing Jars

A simple way to add light and decoration is with candleholders made from jars covered with colored tissue paper.

Supplies
- ☐ glass jar or small vase
- ☐ colored tissue paper: orange, black, green, yellow
- ☐ 1 small candle (such as a tea light)
- ☐ transparent tape
- ☐ ruler
- ☐ pencil
- ☐ scissors

Directions

- Measure the height and circumference of the jar or vase.
- Use the ruler and a pencil to draw lines indicating the size of the piece of tissue paper that needs to be cut.
- In pencil, draw a jack-o'-lantern face or another pattern on the cut tissue paper.
- If you wish, add another layer of tissue paper of a different color to the back of your cut piece. This way, another color will glow through and the candle will not be visible through the cutaway areas.
- Carefully position the tissue paper on the jar or vase and secure it with tape.
- Insert a small candle and carefully light it with a long match.

Hints & ideas

- An alternative is to paint glass jars or bowls. Use glass paints in a variety of colors (e.g., black, orange, white, green, yellow, purple).
- Ensure that the jar or bowl is clean and avoid touching the surface to be painted.
- Trace your preferred pattern onto a piece of tracing paper.
- Cut out the patterns and tape them to the inside of the jar to indicate where you want to paint them.
- Carefully apply the paint. Let each coat dry before adding a new color or layer.
- If you wish, glue on extra decorative accents such as jewels, buttons, sequins or plastic bugs.
- Remove the tracing paper from the inside of the jar.

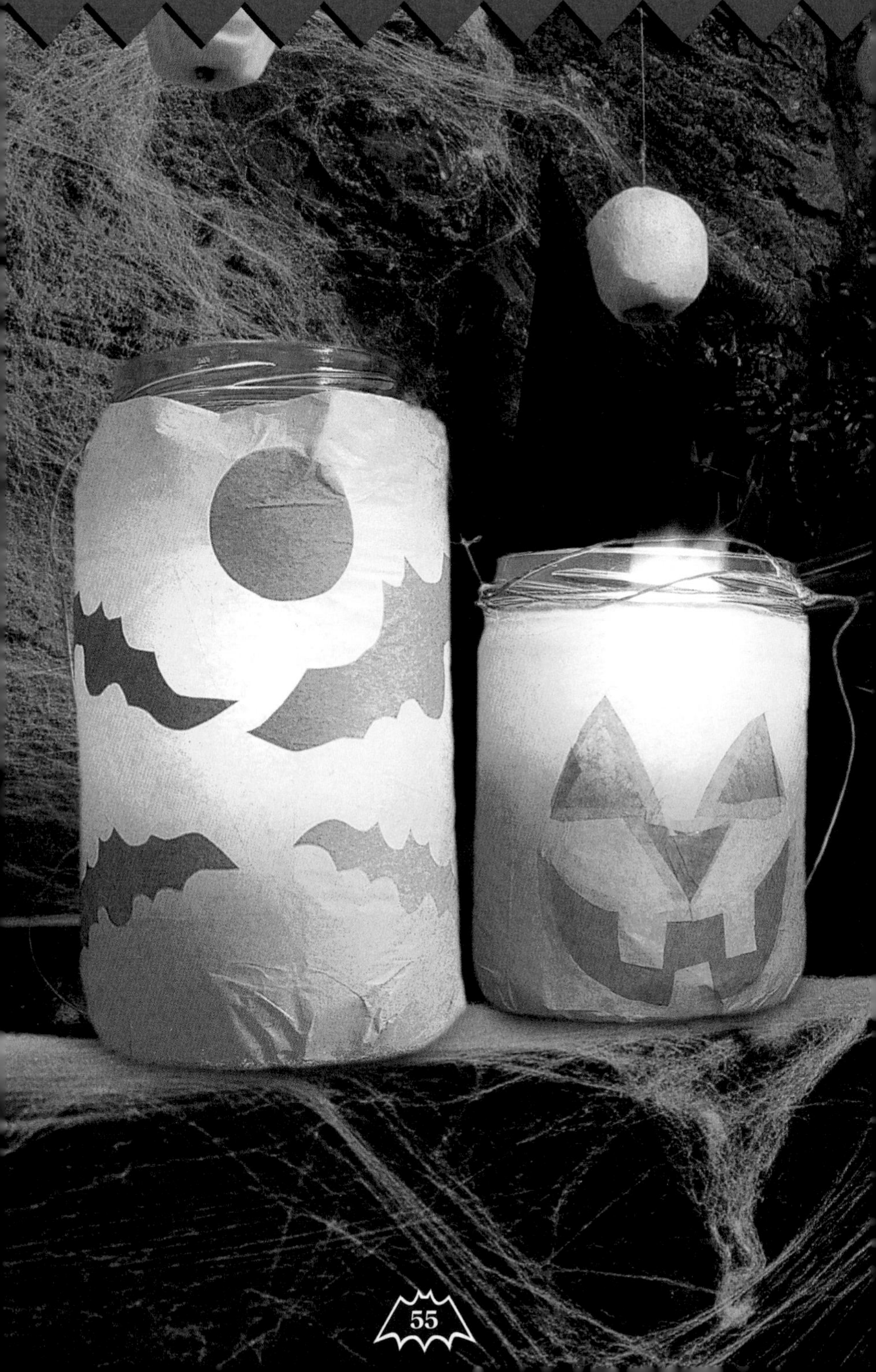

Dangling Heads

Surprise your ghosts by hanging a couple of creepy ghoulish masks in unexpected spots. We chose to hang ours in the bathroom, but another frightening location would be in a closet.

Supplies

- ❑ 2 or 3 frightening masks
- ❑ 8' (2.4 m) of string (or more, depending on the number of masks)
- ❑ fabric—a white bed-sheet or black fabric
- ❑ newspaper
- ❑ scary sign for door (if you're putting the masks in a closet)
- ❑ scissors
- ❑ tape or stapler
- ❑ pushpins

Directions

- Stuff crunched-up newspaper into the masks to make them appear full.
- Cut the string in half if using two masks, in thirds if using three masks.
- Using tape or a stapler, fasten a piece of string to the top of each mask.
- With pushpins, attach the fabric to the wall or the inside of the door frame, creating a backdrop for the masks.
- Use pushpins to secure the other ends of the string to the wall or to the frame at the top of the closet door. Adjust the length of the string if necessary so that masks will dangle at eye level. Trim any remaining string.
- If necessary, tape the backs of the masks to the sheet to prevent them from moving around.
- Close the closet door and attach a creepy sign to the door, such as "Enter at Your Own Risk!" or "Keep Out!"

Hints & ideas

- It is best to use masks that have a full back—in other words, masks that pull over the head. Masks with open backs are difficult to stuff.
- The best effects are achieved with masks that are very frightening or disgusting to look at!
- Consider applying splatters of fake blood (see recipe on page 158) to the fabric or masks for an added effect.

Witch's Hand in Treat Bowl

Combine your treat with a trick! Greet trick-or-treaters at the door with this treat bowl with a twist—a frightening hand poking out from beneath the candy.

Directions

- Fill glove with rice or sand. Tie the opening of the glove closed with an elastic band or twist tie.
- Attach the fake fingernails and paint them with black nail polish.

58

- Paint on a scar or blood splatters with red nail polish.
- Add Halloween rings and use glue to attach small plastic spiders or worms.
- Place the hand inside the bowl or basket and cover it with treats and candies so that the hand appears to be emerging from the treats.

Hints & ideas

- You can make the hand look green by spraying the glove with green shoe dye. Shade the hand by gently patting on black paint.
- Have two hands sticking out from under a couch or chair—it will look as if a witch is trapped underneath!

Hairy Head Plant Pots

Plant some grass or sprouts for hair, paint on a Halloween face and watch your pot come to life!

Directions

- If your pot requires painting, seal it with acrylic paint sealer and then paint it with acrylic paint in your choice of color. Let dry.
- If you have a pattern that you wish to follow, use transfer paper to transfer it to the pot.
- Using accent pens, markers or acrylic paints and a paintbrush, add facial features and other accents such as stitches to the front of the pot.
- Seal with acrylic paint sealer.
- With a glue gun, attach any additional features that you cut out of craft foam: ears, a nose, eyebrows, lips, etc.
- Fill the pot with potting soil and plant the seeds. Then simply wait for the "hair" to grow!
- If you don't have time to grow grass in the pot, use it to hold other potted plants or ornamental gourds instead.

Supplies

- ❏ 1 plant pot, 9–12" (23–30 cm) diameter
- ❏ acrylic paint sealer
- ❏ acrylic paints in a variety of colors
- ❏ accent liner pens or markers: black, white, silver, etc.
- ❏ craft foam in various colors, for facial features
- ❏ potting soil
- ❏ alfalfa seeds, rye grass or other grass seed (see suggestions opposite)
- ❏ paintbrush
- ❏ transfer paper
- ❏ glue gun

Hints & ideas

- Be sure to start the seeds well in advance of Halloween to ensure that the "hair" grows in time.
- Either purchase your pot in the color that you would like the head to be or paint it with acrylic paint.
- You can experiment by growing different types of "hair" for your pots. Try blue fescue ('Elijah Blue'), Sprenger's asparagus fern or rye grass.
- There are many different faces that you can apply to your pots. Use your imagination or try some of the following suggestions:
- **Ghoul or Vampire** Use a silver pot and paint a black face, or use a black pot and paint silver and white facial features and accents. For a vampire, draw on some scary teeth and use red acrylic paint to add a few drops of blood dripping from the mouth. You can also paint or draw a wound and stitch on the ghoul's face.
- **Witch** Use a green pot and glue on a witch's nose for added effect. Glue on a small plastic spider or snake as well, if you wish.
- **Frankenstein's Monster** Add conduit screw connectors to the sides of the head to suggest the monster of Frankenstein. Draw or paint on a couple of stitches.
- **Jack-o'-Lantern** Use an orange pot and add a face with black paint.

Table of Spiders

Put together this simple tablecloth for your dinner or buffet table and it will look as if your table is infested with creepy, crawly spiders!

Supplies

- ☐ 1 piece of tulle fabric to fit your table with a 10–12" (25–35 cm) overhang
- ☐ dozens of plastic spiders
- ☐ craft or fabric scissors
- ☐ needle and thread

Directions

- Cut the fabric to an appropriate size and shape for your table.
- With a needle and thread or sewing machine, hem the piece of fabric.
- Place the fabric on the table. Arrange your place settings.
- Insert each spider's legs into the holes of the fabric. Have some spiders on top of the table and several more hanging from the overhang.

Hints & ideas

- Any remaining tulle fabric can be formed into small decorative ghosts.
- If you don't have time to make the fabric tablecloth, simply scatter plastic spiders and/or other small bugs over your table.

Shrunken Apple Heads

This classic craft is perfect for Halloween. Line up some shrunken heads on a mantel or use them as a creepy accent among the food you are serving.

Supplies

- ☐ apples, fairly large
- ☐ ½ cup (125 ml) lemon juice
- ☐ 2 tsp. (10 ml) salt
- ☐ small knife
- ☐ potato peeler (optional)

Directions

- For each shrunken head, peel an apple. Coat the peeled apple with a mixture of the lemon juice and salt, to prevent browning.
- With a potato peeler or small knife, carve out the features of a face. Make them as spooky or sinister as you like.
- Set the apples aside in a dry place for about 2 weeks. Before the apples harden completely, you can modify their shapes a little.

Hints & ideas

- Individual grains of rice can be poked into the carved mouths to suggest teeth.
- Whole cloves or peppercorns can be poked into the apples for eyes.

Extra Touches

- **Skeleton in the Closet** Frighten guests by hanging a full-size plastic skeleton in one of your closets. Use a black sheet or garbage bag as a backdrop.

Dangling Streamers To form a division between rooms, or to create some mystery by making it difficult for guests to see into a certain room, hang orange and black streamers along the top of a door frame. A simple way to hang these is to first measure and cut the pieces, then staple them along a piece of string that is the width of your doorway. Next, tape or tack the string to the top of the door frame.

Balloons Hanging clusters of black and orange balloons is a simple way to add decoration and color. Consider tying bunches of helium-filled balloons to railings or the backs of chairs. If you have children at your party, each of them can take a couple of balloons home.

Plastic Creatures There are some very realistic-looking plastic snakes, spiders, bugs and rats available at toy stores and novelty stores. Place these throughout your house to spook your guests. Hang snakes from railings or light fixtures, or have a couple of them peeking out from underneath pieces of furniture. Leave a plastic rat on the floor in the bathroom and another on your kitchen counter. Tape plastic spiders to your bathroom mirror or dining room window.

Spider Infestation Drape artificial cobweb throughout your house. Stretch the strands out as much as possible to make the webs look realistic. Hang some across light fixtures and fireplaces, in corners and on bookshelves. Add a few small plastic spiders to some of the webs.

Dazzling Jack-o'-Lanterns & Pumpkins

I t's Halloween—the spookiest night of the year! The most prominent decorations that appear at this time of year are the displays of colorful pumpkins and flickering jack-o'-lanterns. Come October, grocery stores are lined with stacks of pumpkins, and jack-o'-lantern images are found on stickers, books, cakes, jewelry and clothing. For many people, this is a creepily exciting special occasion. Join in the fervor and light up your house and yard with an enviable showcase of pumpkin pageantry!

Origins of the Jack-o'-Lantern

One of the most well-known symbols of Halloween is the jack-o'-lantern. Young trick-or-treaters look forward to Halloween night, when streets are aglow with these twinkling orange creations. Many of us love to create magical displays of jack-o'-lanterns and pumpkins when Halloween approaches, but we don't often think about the roots of this somewhat strange tradition.

The most famous tale of the origin of the jack-o'-lantern is an old Irish legend about a disreputable man named Stingy Jack. When Jack died, he couldn't get into heaven and had played so many tricks on the devil that he wasn't even permitted to enter hell. The devil forced him to walk the dark night for eternity, with only a piece of burning coal to light his way. Jack carried the coal in a hollowed-out turnip. He became known to the Irish as "Jack of the Lantern," later shortened to "Jack o'Lantern."

This legend evolved into a tradition in Ireland and Scotland of setting jack-o'-lanterns—carved from turnips, rutabagas and even large beets—in windows or on doorsteps. People believed that these lanterns would frighten away Jack and other sinister spirits thought to roam the earth at night. Immigrants later brought this eerie legend and tradition to North America, where they found that pumpkins, which are native to our continent, made great lanterns. Other North Americans embraced the tradition as well, and as a result, people have now been carving jack-o'-lanterns for centuries!

Pumpkin Trivia

- A pumpkin is a fruit, not a vegetable. It is a member of the gourd family (Cucurbitaceae), which includes squash, cucumbers, melons and gherkins. Many of these are also used as Halloween and harvest-season decorations.
- Pumpkins are native to the western hemisphere and have been grown in North America for about 5000 years.
- Pumpkin-growing competitions are held across North America, and the winners often top 1000 pounds (the winning *pumpkins*, that is!).
- The most common varieties of pumpkin used for carving jack-o'-lanterns are Trick-or-Treat, Spirit and Connecticut Field. All these varieties yield edible seeds.
- Pumpkins are low in fat, calories and sodium, and they are a good source of vitamins A and B, potassium, protein, fiber and iron.
- Pumpkin seeds taste great added to salads and stuffings, baked into breads, or roasted and eaten as a snack. They can even be covered in chocolate or baked into a brittle. See our recipe for **Roasted Pumpkin Seeds** (sidebar).
- Children love to thread pumpkin seeds together to form necklaces. These strands can also make great decorative touches. See **Pumpkin Seed Jewelry** (page 121).

Roasted Pumpkin Seeds

To roast 1½ cups (325 ml) of pumpkin seeds, scoop the seeds out of the pumpkin and remove the pulp from the seeds. (Soaking the seeds in water for about an hour makes this task easier.) Rinse the seeds well and pat dry with a dishtowel. Mix the seeds in a bowl with 2 tsp. (10 ml) vegetable oil or melted butter, and salt to taste. Spray a baking sheet with nonstick cooking spray, and spread the seeds on the baking sheet. Bake at 300° F (150° C) for about 30 minutes, stirring occasionally, until the seeds are dry and golden brown.

Inspiring Ideas for Jack-o'-Lanterns

The most popular way to dress up a Halloween pumpkin is to carve it into a jack-o'-lantern with a fearsome face. However, there are many alternatives to simply cutting out triangular eyes and a zigzag mouth. As this tradition has evolved, people have come up with dozens of creative carving concepts. Let your imagination run wild and use these ideas to get you started!

- For ready-to-use designs and tips on carving a great jack-o'-lantern, look for Ghost House Books' *Pumpkin Carving* (see last page of this book for price and ordering information).
- For carving designs, try swirls, vertical stripes or short words.
- Put some nuggets of dry ice inside a carved pumpkin for a spooky effect. (Note: exercise caution when using dry ice. We recommend not using dry ice around children.)

- Hang one or two lanterns with traditional jack-o'-lantern faces in a dark area of your yard to give the scary impression of floating faces.
- Place three pumpkins on top of each other, like a snowman, and carve the top one.
- Hang an assortment of patterned jack-o'-lanterns from plant hangers or hooks. Use fairly small pumpkins, and carve simple designs into them. Cut lengths of rope or thick twine for hanging each pumpkin. Cut a small hole on each side of the pumpkin, just below the opening at the top. Pull a length of rope through at each side and tie knots to secure. Place one to three small candles in each pumpkin, and then hang the pumpkins from lanterns or plant stands.

Punched-out Pumpkin

stunning alternative to a carved
k-o'-lantern, this version sends
ams of light shining out
rough dozens of drilled holes.

Directions

Cut an opening in the bottom of the
pumpkin. Scoop out the seeds and
fiber from the pumpkin, using a
spoon or ice cream scoop.

If you wish, spray the entire
pumpkin with black spray paint. Let dry. If you don't want
to use spray paint, you can still get a great effect by simply mak
the holes in the pumpkin, as we did (see photo).

With the drill, drill holes all over the
pumpkin. You can follow a fairly
uniform pattern or drill the
holes randomly.

Another way to make the
holes is to use a potato
peeler that has a
serrated edge. Push
the knife in and twist
it, cutting out a hole.

Place a candle or
small floodlight or
flashlight
underneath the
pumpkin.

Supplies

- ❑ large fresh pumpkin
- ❑ black spray paint (optional)
- ❑ candle or small floodlight or flashlight
- ❑ knife or carving tool
- ❑ large spoon or ice cream scoop
- ❑ electric drill and drill bit or potato peeler with serrated edge

Painted Pumpkins

A safe alternative to carving pumpkins is to paint them. Let the many available sizes and shapes of pumpkins inspire you.

Supplies
- ❑ pumpkin
- ❑ acrylic paints
- ❑ permanent markers

Directions

- Draw an outline of your design on your pumpkin, sketching it in pencil first if you wish. Some interesting designs are stripes, checkerboard designs, swirls or polka dots.
- Use acrylic paints to complete the design.
- Accent with metallic or colored permanent markers.

Hints & ideas

- You might want to first spray paint the entire pumpkin with a base color. For example, spray paint a pumpkin gray and paint on a ghoul's face complete with stitches, or spray paint it green, glue on a witch's nose, yarn hair and hat, and paint on features.

Variation

Decorated Gourds

- Use paint, metallic permanent markers or glitter pens and glitter glue to brighten up gourds. Inspired by the shape and size of the gourds, we drew a wizard on one gourd and a spider web and spider on another.
  - Decorative patterns such as swirls, vines, stripes, diamonds, spider's webs, bats or even tiny pumpkin shapes transform a gourd into a decorative element, as spooky or playful as you like.
  - If painting a face on your pumpkin or gourd, apply crazy-looking craft eyes for a whimsical touch.

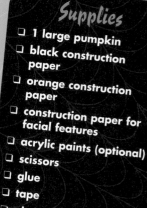

Sinister Spider Pumpkin

You can decorate a pumpkin to look like pretty much anything—why not try an eight-legged, creepy spider?

Directions

- To create 8 jointed legs out of the black and orange construction paper, first make 24 black tubes. Cut 24 pieces of the black construction paper, each 5" × 6" (13 cm × 15 cm). Roll each piece of paper lengthwise into a tube about 6" (15 cm) long and 1" (2.5 cm) in diameter. Secure the roll with tape.
- Create 16 orange tubes, each slightly larger in circumference than the black tubes (the black tubes need to be able to fit inside the orange tubes). For each orange tube, you will need a rectangle of orange construction paper 4" × 5" (10 cm × 13 cm). Roll each rectangle to create a tube about 4" (10 cm) long and 1½–2" (4–5 cm) in diameter. Secure with tape.
- Create 8 legs by putting a black tube inside each end of an orange tube. Attach the legs to the spider with pins or flat-headed thumbtacks.
- Cut feet out of construction paper and glue feet onto the spider's legs.
- Cut the spider's features out of construction paper and glue the features onto the pumpkin or paint the features on.

Hints & ideas

- For an enhanced effect, drape fake cobweb around the spider pumpkin and add a couple of small plastic bugs to the web.

Elegantly Decorated Pumpkins

See pumpkins in a new light. Far from sinister, these pumpkins look positively elegant in your house or on your porch.

Beribboned Pumpkin

Directions

- Choose ribbon colors to contrast with the orange of the pumpkin or to coordinate with a color scheme you've already established. You can use one color of ribbon, a patterned ribbon or (as we did) one narrower ribbon over another wider one in a contrasting color.

Supplies

- ❏ pumpkin
- ❏ ribbon or ribbons in various colors and widths
- ❏ small pins, flat thumb-tacks or tape.

- Cut the ribbon to a length that will allow you to wrap the ribbon pieces up from the bottom of the pumpkin to the top, preferably leaving some ribbon to dangle or curl at the top.
- Secure the ribbon with small dressmaker pins or tape.

Hints & ideas

- You will find fabric ribbon easier to work with than gift-wrapping ribbon.
- Paint your pumpkin before attaching the ribbon if you like.
- Add a touch of whimsy by using polka dot or plaid ribbon.

Bejeweled Pumpkin

Directions

- Adhere the gems or jewelry pieces to the surface of the pumpkin. Create a pattern or place the gems randomly.
- Accent with swirls of black or metallic marker if you wish.
- Attach draping silk leaves to add another interesting element to your decorated pumpkin.

Supplies

- ❏ pumpkin
- ❏ assorted plastic or metal gems or jewelry
- ❏ silk leaves to accent (optional)
- ❏ permanent markers (optional)
- ❏ glue

Hints & ideas

- A dollar store or craft store is a great source for plastic gems.
- Deck your pumpkin out according to a theme, depending on what kind of gems are available.

Assorted Decorated Pumpkins

Put on a parade by decorating pumpkins with glitter, metallic pens, vegetables, jewels, pushpins or anything your heart desires. The sky is the limit! Come up with your own ideas for decorating this popular Halloween fruit or try some of the following suggestions:

Dressed to Thrill Dress your pumpkin up with hats, scarves, hair, braids, feathers. Glue on ears and noses of cardboard, gourds, fabric, vegetables. Set a jack-o'-lantern head on a body made with stuffed clothes and boots. Add whiskers made from wire or cut from a broom, and fake sideburns. *Note:* be sure that the items you select are safe choices and that they are not too close to the candle flame. When in doubt, use a flashlight rather than a candle.

Veggie Version Form a crazy face on your pumpkin by using toothpicks to fasten on a variety of vegetables. Determine the placement of the facial features and then carefully push toothpicks into the pumpkin wall. Attach the veggies to the tips of the toothpicks.

Try using cucumber and radish slices or olives for eyes, green beans for eyebrows or whiskers, a carrot for a nose, red pepper slices for lips, peas or garlic cloves for teeth, cabbage leaves or broccoli florets for hair. Raid your fridge and be creative!

Bug-Infested Surprise Stick a variety of plastic creepy crawlies—such as spiders, lizards, small snakes and cockroaches—on a pumpkin. If you want, you can first spray paint the pumpkin gray or dull green to suggest age and mold. Use black, green and silver markers to accent and give the appearance of spider webs and grass. A snake or bug climbing out of a hole cut in the pumpkin looks suggestively sinister!

Stars and Moons Buy some glow-in-the-dark stars and moons and stick them to a small pumpkin. Place it on your porch or in a bathroom, and every time it becomes dark, guests and visitors will be in for a glowing surprise. Alternatively, you can draw or paint stars, moons and swirling clouds using metallic paints, glitter pens or metallic markers.

Words to Ward Off Spirits Paint a large "BOO!" or write "Beware!" in drippy paint letters. Use glue to adhere messages made from alphabet macaroni letters to your pumpkin. Carefully paint the tops of the letters with black or metallic acrylic paint. Try a verse from your favorite scary poem or a couple of lines from a creepy horror movie, or simply write Halloween greetings. Accent with swirling designs in black or metallic pen or decorative dabs of acrylic paint.

Metallic Masterpieces You can create some uniquely decorated pumpkins with metallic paints, wire and even such items as grommets and eyelets. Fashion curling vines from thin copper wire and twirl them around the pumpkin's stem. Spray paint leaves with gold metallic paint and gently fasten them to the stem with glue or by fastening them to the copper wire. Another interesting idea is to cover a pumpkin with gold and copper eyelets. Simply push them into the surface of the pumpkin and, if you wish, accent with spirals drawn with metallic markers.

Devilishly Delectable Treats

This is the spookiest, scariest time of the year, and your guests will expect food that is suitably sinister and terrifyingly tasty. Preparing a Halloween feast doesn't have to be a harrowing experience for the host—often all it involves is giving ordinary dishes a decidedly gruesome or spooky twist! Make your famished friends' blood run cold with these frighteningly delectable recipes, gruesome goodies and bewitching beverages. They are sure to add a blood-curdling touch to your Halloween festivities!

Crispy Roasted Bones

Not only are these bones a snap to make, they're also sure to be a hit with guests young and old.

Directions

- Preheat oven according to the breadstick package directions. Line a cookie sheet with foil or parchment paper.
- Unroll the breadstick dough and separate the pieces. Roll each piece slightly to extend its length to 10–12" (25–30 cm).
- Cut each breadstick in half, creating two shorter sticks. At each end, carefully tie a knot so that the breadsticks resemble small bones or dog treats. Place them on the lined cookie sheet.
- In a bowl, whisk the egg white with a fork or wire whisk.
- Using a pastry brush, apply a light coat of egg white to the tops of the bones.
- Sprinkle the bones with your choice of toppings—sesame seeds, poppy seeds and/or Parmesan cheese.
- Following the package directions, bake the breadsticks until they are lightly toasted (approximately 10–12 minutes).
- Recipe yields about 12 bones.

Hints & ideas

- For a tasty alternative that children in particular will love, sprinkle the bones with sugar mixed with some cinnamon.

Wicked Wiener Fingers

Create a chilling collection of cut-off fingers and lay them on a bed of lettuce for a dreadfully shocking display.

Supplies

- several wieners, cooked if desired
- red peppers or cherry tomatoes
- cream cheese
- lettuce
- ketchup or salsa

Directions

- Cut the wieners in half crosswise. Make slits to resemble knuckles. At the tips of the wiener halves, cut out small wedges on which to fasten "fingernails."
- Cut red peppers or small tomatoes into fingernail-sized pieces.
- Spread some cream cheese on the fingernail pieces and adhere them to the tips of the wieners.
- Serve the fingers on a bed of lettuce with a stack of toothpicks for easy handling. Provide a bowl of ketchup or salsa for dipping.

Hints & ideas

- Dip the cut ends of the wieners into ketchup to suggest blood (see picture).
- Another sinister way to display Wicked Wiener Fingers is to have them sticking haphazardly out of the top of a pumpkin. Insert toothpicks into the top of a small pumpkin and then attach the fingers to the other ends of the picks. Give the pumpkin a jack-o'-lantern face with vegetable pieces or a black marker.

Eerie Eyeballs

These deviled-egg eyeballs make a tasty treat, if your horrified guests are brave enough to pop them into their mouths!

Supplies

- [ ] 24 green olives with pimientos
- [ ] 1 dozen eggs
- [ ] ½ cup (125 ml) mayonnaise
- [ ] 1 tsp. (5 ml) prepared mustard
- [ ] ½ tsp. (2.5 ml) salt
- [ ] red gel icing
- [ ] lettuce

Directions

- Lay olives on paper towels to allow the juice to drain off. Cut the olives in half crosswise.
- Set eggs in a large pot and cover them with cold water. Bring to a boil and cook for 1 minute.
- Remove from heat, cover and let stand for 15 minutes.
- Drain the water and run cold water over the eggs.
- Peel the cool eggs, holding them under cold running water if necessary to help loosen the shells.
- Cut eggs in half crosswise (cutting them crosswise rather than lengthwise will make them look rounder, like eyes). Slice a small portion off the bottom of the halves so that they will sit on a plate.
- With a spoon, gently scoop out the yolks and place them in a mixing bowl.
- Use a fork to mash the yolks. Next, add the mayonnaise, mustard and salt, and mix together until the mixture forms a paste.
- Spoon the mixture back into the egg whites.
- Set one olive in the center of each egg and draw bloodshot veins with red gel icing.
- Cover carefully and refrigerate until ready to serve. Serve on a bed of lettuce.

Hints & ideas

- For added flavor, mix some cream cheese in with the mayonnaise.
  - A particularly unnerving way to display the eyeballs is to fill the sections of an egg carton with alfalfa sprouts and set an Eerie Eyeball into each section.

Variation

- **Revolting Radish Eyeballs** Peel small radishes, leaving thin strips of red skin on to look like bloody veins. Using a small knife or vegetable peeler, carefully scoop out a hole in each radish. Insert a green olive with pimiento into each hole. These eyeballs can also be frozen into ice cubes and used in martinis and other beverages.

Jack-o'-Lantern Dip

Serve your spinach dip in a delightfully different way—inside a large round loaf of bread cut to resemble a jeering jack-o'-lantern.

Directions

- In a mixing bowl, thoroughly combine mayonnaise, sour cream and soup or dressing mix. Cover and refrigerate.
- Allow spinach to thaw. Once thawed, drain off excess water and blot with paper towels.
- Add spinach, green onions, cheddar cheese, water chestnuts and garlic to the mixture. Mix well, cover and return to refrigerator.

- Use a sharp knife to cut the top off the loaf of bread. Ensure that the hole is large enough that the dip will be easy to reach.
- Remove the bread from the inside of the loaf, tearing it into small pieces. Be sure to leave a crust on the bread that is at least 1" (2.5 cm) thick.
- Carve a jack-o'-lantern face into the side of the bread crust. Be careful not to carve too deeply, or the dip will seep out from the holes.
- Fill the bread crust with dip and serve with the pieces of bread.

Hints & ideas

- Make the dip several hours in advance or even overnight, and refrigerate in a covered bowl until ready to serve.
- If you don't think you will have enough bread for dipping, either cut up additional pieces from a loaf of French bread or have a supply of crackers on hand.

Supplies

- ❑ 1 round bread loaf (suggestions: French, pumpernickel)
- ❑ 1 cup (250 ml) mayonnaise
- ❑ 1 cup (250 ml) sour cream
- ❑ 1 package vegetable soup mix or ranch dressing mix
- ❑ one 12-oz. (300 g) box frozen chopped spinach
- ❑ ¼ cup (60 ml) green onions, finely chopped
- ❑ 1 cup (250 ml) cheddar cheese, grated
- ❑ 1 small can of water chestnuts, sliced (optional)
- ❑ 1 to 3 crushed garlic cloves (optional)

Beastly Buns

Satisfy the hunger of famished fiends and ghoulish guests by serving them buns decorated with ferocious vegetable faces!

Directions

- Cut open the buns. On each bun, add some mayonnaise and mustard, sandwich meat and a slice of cheese.
- From this point on, let your creative juices flow to make blood-curdling buns with frightful faces and monstrous mouths! Some ideas are listed on the next page.
- Use toothpicks to attach the vegetables to the bun when necessary.

Supplies

- ☐ buns
- ☐ cold cuts or other sandwich toppings
- ☐ slices of cheese
- ☐ mayonnaise
- ☐ mustard
- ☐ lettuce
- ☐ assorted vegetables (cucumber slices, broccoli florets, alfalfa sprouts, radishes, olives, carrots, beans, green onions, pieces of red and canned corn, red and green bell peppers, tomatoes, cocktail onions, celery, cauliflower)

Hints & ideas

- A tomato slice peeking out, a slice of salami or a strip of red pepper can become a tongue.
- Teeth can be made with rows of corn pieces, a jagged piece of cut cucumber or red pepper, or rows of olives or cocktail onions.
- Use long pieces of green onion or chives as spindly spider legs.
- Make ears from carrots, beans, pepper slices or pieces of celery.
- Use broccoli florets, rows of green beans or tufts of alfalfa sprouts as hair.
- Create creepy eyes with cucumber slices that have olives or radishes for pupils, slices of carrot, radishes with pimiento centers or cherry tomatoes.
- Noses can be made from anything—a piece of carrot, a bean, a radish or even a piece of cauliflower.

Spooky Sandwiches

Make ordinary sandwiches spooktacular by using cookie cutters to fashion them into horrendous Halloween shapes!

Directions

- In a bowl, mix together tuna, mayonnaise or yogurt, celery, green onion, curry powder, mustard, salt and pepper.
- Carefully cut the bread pieces with the cookie cutters. Ensure that you cut the shapes in pairs.
- Assemble the sandwiches.
- Spread the tops of the sandwiches with cream cheese if desired, and garnish with two slices of olives to look like eyes.

Hints & ideas

- You can also make these sandwiches using chicken or egg salad, cold cuts and cheese, or even peanut butter and jam.
- If you are serving several different types of sandwiches, consider using a different cookie cutter for each type so that guests can tell them apart more easily.

Supplies

- ❏ 2 cans of water-packed tuna, drained
- ❏ ½ cup (125 ml) mayonnaise or plain yogurt
- ❏ ½ cup (125 ml) celery, chopped finely
- ❏ ¼ cup (60 ml) green onion, chopped finely
- ❏ ½ tsp. (2.5 ml) curry powder (optional)
- ❏ 1 tsp. (5 ml) prepared honey mustard
- ❏ salt and pepper to taste
- ❏ 20 slices of bread with crusts removed
- ❏ whipped cream cheese (optional)
- ❏ black olive slices (optional)
- ❏ Halloween cookie cutters (e.g., ghosts, pumpkins)

Caterpillar Sandwich

This long, crawling sandwich serves several hungry ghouls, and it makes a creepy display on a buffet table!

Directions

- Cut the bread in half lengthwise, creating two long halves of bread. Fill with toppings, then reassemble the loaf.
- Stick two olives on toothpicks and insert them at one end. These are the eyes of the caterpillar.
- Insert two small, thin pieces of red pepper as the caterpillar's antennae.
- Cut the onion into slices, separate the slices into rings and cut each ring in half. Insert half-rings along each side of the sandwich, letting them dangle out to be the caterpillar's legs.
- Using a piece of toothpick or some cream cheese, attach a piece of red pepper as the tongue.

Freaky Pizza Faces

Have witches and goblins decorate their own pumpkin or monster faces on small pizzas, or serve a colorful selection of your own creations.

Directions

- Preheat oven to the temperature indicated on the pizza box.
- Cut vegetables into desired shapes and decorate the pizzas with freakish or friendly faces. Give them eyes, ears, noses, teeth, lips and even eyebrows or hair.
- Bake according to package directions.

Supplies

- ❑ small frozen cheese pizzas
- ❑ assortment of toppings (red and green bell peppers, broccoli, pineapple, tomatoes, radishes, olives, canned corn, pepperoni slices, green onions, etc.)

Olive Hands

A pair of horrifying frozen hands sticking out of a bowlful of olives is sure to make your guests' flesh crawl.

Supplies

- ❑ 1 pair of small latex gloves
- ❑ two 14-oz. (398 ml) cans of jumbo black olives

Directions

- Wash gloves well. Fill both latex gloves with water and tie each glove in a knot at the end. Freeze until solid.
- Remove the gloves from the freezer. Do not peel the latex gloves off the frozen hands. Add an olive to the tip of each finger. Place the gloves in a bowl with the fingers pointing upwards.
- Pour the remaining olives into the bowl so that they surround the gloves and hide the tied ends.

Witch's Hat Cookies

Ghoulish guests, both young and young at heart, will enjoy munching on these chocolaty hats. They will be surprised to find a hidden stash of candy inside each hat, too.

Directions

- Fill the resealable bag with some chocolate icing. Seal the bag, and then cut a small end off one corner. Set aside.
- Fill each ice cream cone with small candies.
- Take the bag of icing and pipe some along the bottom edge of each cone.
- Press a cookie onto the icing-coated rim of each cone, and then gently turn over so that the cone is now upside down.
- Decorate each cone with icing or by applying small candies, sticking them on with additional icing.

Hints & ideas

- Flatten out large green and yellow gumdrops with a rolling pin on a sugared surface. Cut into ¼" (6.5 mm) strips. Press green strips around brim of hat and use smaller pieces of yellow strips to form a buckle. Press onto hat.
- Trim one side of a cone a bit so that the hat sits at an angle.
- Have children create and decorate these witches' hats as a party activity. They can then take them home to enjoy.

Supplies

- ❑ one 14-oz. (450 g) can of prepared chocolate icing
- ❑ 20 chocolate or sugar ice cream cones (must be pointy, not flat-bottomed)
- ❑ assorted small candies (e.g., candy corn, orange and brown candy-covered chocolate pieces, etc.)
- ❑ 20 chocolate wafer cookies or chocolate-covered digestive cookies
- ❑ large yellow and green gumdrops (optional)
- ❑ 1 resealable plastic bag

Spider Cupcakes

Give these cupcakes spindly spider legs and googly eyes. Your guests will take great pleasure out of devouring these creepy creatures.

Supplies

- ❏ one 16-oz. (510 g) box cake mix
- ❏ one 14-oz. (450 g) can prepared icing
- ❏ orange food coloring (optional)
- ❏ thin licorice strings
- ❏ large black or green gumdrops

Directions

- Make the cupcakes, following package directions.
- Mix orange food coloring into the vanilla icing, if desired.
- Frost the cupcakes.
- Push eight 2"-long (5 cm-long) pieces of licorice into the center of each cupcake. These will form the legs. Set a large black or green gumdrop in the center to form the spider's body. Add eyes made from small bits of leftover frosting, or attach small candies with frosting.

Hints & ideas

- If you like, make your favorite cupcake and frosting recipes instead of store-bought varieties.

Variation

- **Spiderweb Cupcakes** Use white icing. Using black decorator gel icing or an icing pen, draw an uninterrupted swirl on the top of the cupcake. Then take a toothpick and at intervals gently drag the pattern outwards from the center to the edges to form a web effect.
- **Eyeball Cupcakes** Use white icing. Carefully draw red veins on with red decorator gel icing or red food coloring. Add a maraschino cherry or red gumdrop in the center and top it with a blob of black decorator gel icing.

Gruesome Maggot Cookies

Label a serving tray of these goodies "Gruesome Maggot Cookies" or "Wormy Crisps" and really unnerve your guests!

Supplies
- one 6-oz. (188 g) package butterscotch chips
- 1 cup (250 ml) salted peanuts
- 3 cups (750 ml) chow mein noodles

Directions

- In a saucepan, melt the butterscotch pieces over low heat, stirring constantly. (Or microwave them on medium-low heat for about one minute. Stir well. If necessary, continue to heat the chips gradually until they are melted, stirring them each time you heat them.)
- Remove the butterscotch mixture from heat and stir in the peanuts and chow mein noodles.
- Drop the mixture by teaspoonfuls onto waxed paper and let them cool.

Recipes

Witch's Finger Cookies

There's something deliciously depraved about munching on these sweet, crunchy fingers.

Supplies

- 2½ cups (625 ml) flour
- 1 tsp. (5 ml) baking powder
- 1 tsp. (5 ml) salt
- 1 cup (250 ml) butter, softened
- 1 cup (250 ml) sugar
- 1 egg
- 1 tsp. (5 ml) almond extract
- 1 tsp. (5 ml) vanilla extract
- ½ cup (125 ml) whole blanched almonds
- red or green food coloring and/or decorating gel
- clean small paintbrush

Directions

- Preheat oven to 325° F (160° C).
- Combine flour, baking powder and salt in a mixing bowl.
- In another large bowl, beat together butter, sugar, egg, and almond and vanilla extracts.
- Beat in dry ingredients until dough is well mixed.
- Cover and refrigerate dough for 30 minutes.
- Working with one-quarter of the dough at a time (keep remaining dough refrigerated), roll small balls of dough (about two large spoonfuls) into finger shapes. Squeeze the dough in a couple of spots to form the appearance of knuckles. Make the cookies narrower than you think they should be, as they will spread during baking.
- Press an almond firmly onto one end of each finger to form fingernails. If you want to paint them, use a clean brush and apply red or green food coloring that has been diluted with water.
- Place cookies on a lightly greased cookie sheet and bake for 20–25 minutes or until golden. Let cool for 2–3 minutes.
- Remove the cookies from the cookie sheet and set them on a wire rack to cool.

Hints & ideas

- You can lift up the almonds on the baked cookies and squeeze some red decorating gel under each nail. Press the almond back in place so that the gel oozes out.

- Consider adding green food coloring to the dough so the fingers look green.

- You can also make Witch's Toe Cookies. Simply shape the cookies somewhat shorter and chubbier.

Spiderweb Brownies

Decorate these chocolaty brownies with a sticky web. Sweet-toothed witches and goblins will be eager to indulge.

Supplies

- ❏ 4 squares unsweetened baking chocolate
- ❏ ½ cup (125 ml) butter or margarine
- ❏ 2 cups (500 ml) sugar
- ❏ 3 eggs
- ❏ 1 tsp. (5 ml) vanilla
- ❏ 1 cup (250 ml) unbleached flour
- ❏ 1 cup (250 ml) coarsely chopped nuts
- ❏ one 14-oz. (450 g) can vanilla icing
- ❏ 1 square semi-sweet baking chocolate, melted

Directions

- Preheat oven to 350° F (175° C), or 325° F (160° C) if using a glass baking dish.
- Line a 13" × 9" (33 cm × 23 cm) baking pan with foil, extending the foil over the edges so that the brownies can be lifted out after they are baked. Grease the foil.
- In a small saucepan over low heat or in the microwave, melt the unsweetened chocolate and butter. Stir until chocolate is completely melted. Let cool.
- Stir the sugar into the chocolate mixture until it is well mixed. Mix in eggs and vanilla.
- Stir in the flour and nuts until well mixed.
- Spread the mixture into the pan.
- Bake for 30–35 minutes or until a toothpick inserted in the center comes out with sticky crumbs. Be careful not to overcook.
- Once the brownies have cooled, lift them out of the pan. Remove the foil and transfer the brownies to a serving tray.
- Ice with vanilla icing.
- Use melted semi-sweet chocolate to create a web pattern.

Hints & ideas

- You can use a store-bought brownie or cake mix and top with marshmallow creme and drizzled chocolate.
- An easy way to drizzle chocolate is to insert the square into a resealable plastic bag, microwave it on high for about 30 seconds, and then knead the bag to melt the chocolate completely. Next, cut a small hole at the tip of one corner of the bag and gently squeeze the chocolate out of the hole.

Sugar Cookies

Bring store-bought sugar cookies to life with orange icing and candies. Children love to decorate these themselves.

Directions

- Mix orange food coloring into vanilla icing until it is bright orange.
- Spread icing onto sugar cookies.
- Use your imagination and decorate the cookies with a variety of small candy pieces. Make jack-o'-lantern faces with candy corn, tiny jellybeans and other assorted candies. Try pieces of green jujube as leaves or brown candies as stems.

Hints & ideas

- If you prefer, use your own favorite recipe and make sugar cookies from scratch. Be sure to let them cool completely before icing them.
- You can also make some of the dough into bone-shaped cookies by rolling the dough and cutting it with dog-bone-shaped cookie cutters (often available at pet supply stores).

Caramel and Marshmallow Apples

This classic Halloween treat can be left plain or decorated with candy or crushed peanuts.

Directions

- Line a baking sheet with greased waxed paper or parchment paper and set aside.
- Wash the apples. Push a craft stick into the top of each one.
- Combine caramels, marshmallows and water in a large saucepan.
- Cook over medium heat, stirring constantly, until the mixture has melted. Let it cool slightly.
- Carefully dip and coat the apples in the melted caramel mixture. Place the apples on the waxed paper.
- If desired, decorate the apples with candy corn, nuts, licorice bits or other candies.
- Refrigerate apples until they are firm.

Hints & ideas

- Another decorating idea is to drizzle melted chocolate over the caramel apples.
- If you are serving the apples to young children, consider cutting them into pieces first.

Wormy Plant Pot

Make a terra-cotta plant pot appear to be crawling with wiggling worms! Guests will be pleased to discover that the contents of this bug-infested pot are actually deliciously edible.

Directions

- If the pot has a hole in the bottom, seal the hole by lining the bottom with a foil-wrapped circle of cardboard.
- Prepare the chocolate cake according to package directions.
- Once the cake has cooled, scoop it out into a bowl. Mix in the pudding so that the mixture is sticky and moist.
- Mix in some gummy worms and scoop the mixture into the terra-cotta pot.
- Stick a few more gummy worms out of the top of the mixture, and hang some over the sides of the pot.

Hints & ideas

- Use a prepared chocolate cake instead of baking a cake.
- A simpler variation that children love to make is to alternate layers of crushed chocolate sandwich cookies with layers of chocolate pudding in a clear plastic cup. Make the top layer one of crushed cookies, which resemble dirt, and add a few gummy worms.

Bewitching Beverages

Enhance your party by extending the Halloween theme to the drinks you serve. You can easily set the mood by using Halloween dishes and glassware, and just a few extra touches will make even ordinary drinks look a little sinister. Use our recipes and suggestions to enhance the macabre mood.

- Freeze **Revolting Radish Eyeballs** (see page 83) into ice cubes and place them in martinis or glasses of punch. Also, see the ideas for creepy ice cubes on pages 107–110.
- Carefully insert a large glass bowl inside a carved jack-o'-lantern. Then fill the bowl with punch and you'll have a haunting Halloween cauldron! You can even decorate the jack-o'-lantern by gluing on a few creepy plastic lizards and spiders.
- Use green- or orange-tinted plastic glasses for your party beverages.
- Put raisins and/or blueberries into a glass before adding your drink. They will float to the top, suggesting swimming bugs.
- Decorate party glasses by having a gummy worm or snake crawling out of the glass, and use straws in Halloween colors.
- Decorate plain glasses with a spiderweb pattern. Use a white accent pen to draw a spiderweb design on the outside of a glass.

Mysterious Bug Punch

This punch appears to have dead insects floating in it!

Directions

- Place a couple of raisins in each section of an ice cube tray. Add water and freeze until solid.
- In a punch bowl, combine all the juices and sugar if desired. Add the "bug" ice cubes and serve.

Hints & ideas

- Keep the juices cold until you are ready to serve the punch.
- To ensure the ice cubes are clear, use distilled water, preferably first boiled and then cooled. Otherwise, the ice cubes could turn cloudy as they freeze.

Supplies

For ice cubes:
- ❑ 24–36 raisins

For punch:
- ❑ 4 pints (2 liters) cranberry juice
- ❑ 2½ cups (625 ml) peach juice
- ❑ 1 cup (250 ml) fresh lemon or lime juice
- ❑ 2 cups (500 ml) orange juice
- ❑ sugar to taste

Frozen Critter Cubes

These will make your guests think twice about taking a sip of their party punch!

Supplies

- ☐ plastic bugs (16)
- ☐ ice cube tray

Directions

- Clean the plastic bugs with dish soap in warm water; rinse well. Place a bug (we used flies) in each section of ice cube tray.
- Cover each bug with water. Make certain a bug remains in each tray section. Place ice cube tray in freezer and allow cubes to freeze solid.

Hints & ideas

- These cubes are not a good choice for young children, as the melted cubes could present a choking hazard. Use caution and warn your guests that the bugs cannot be swallowed.
- To prevent your ice cubes from getting cloudy, you can use distilled water for the cubes. It works best if you boil the distilled water first to ensure clear, yet buggy, ice cubes.

Wormy Frozen Hands

Keep your punch cold with these frightful floating hands!

Directions

- Thoroughly wash the gloves. Rinse them well and let dry.
- Line a cookie sheet with paper towels.
- In a pitcher, mix the beverage mix, sugar and water according to package directions. If you would like to alter the color of the mixture, add some drops of food coloring.
- Carefully pour the mix into the gloves. If you desire, add a few gummy worms to the gloves. Seal them tightly with twist ties or elastic bands.
- Gently lay the gloves on the cookie sheet and place in the freezer until frozen solid.
- When you are ready to serve your punch, cut the gloves off the hands and place the frozen hands in the punch bowl.

Supplies

- ❑ 1 pair disposable gloves, preferably nonlatex and nonpowdered
- ❑ 1 package powdered beverage mix (preferably red, orange or green)
- ❑ 1 cup (250 ml) sugar (or according to drink mix directions)
- ❑ food coloring (optional)
- ❑ a few gummy worms (optional)
- ❑ 2 twist ties or elastic bands

Hints & ideas

- You might want to make more hands than you'll really need in case the fingers break after they're frozen.
- Make sure that the flavor of beverage mix you choose will complement the flavors in your punch.
- Try to select a beverage mix in a contrasting color to your punch, so that it shows up easily.

Eyeball Ice Cubes

A delightfully disgusting idea is to create ice cubes that look as if they have decaying eyeballs in them!

Directions

- Peel the skin off of the grapes.
- Fill the ice cube container with water and add a few drops of green food coloring to each section.
- Once you have achieved the desired shade of green in the water, place a peeled grape in each section of the tray. Freeze until the cubes are solid and then serve in your beverage of choice.

Hints & ideas

- The eyeballs are most easily visible in a fairly clear beverage (such as a ginger ale and white grape juice punch).

Supplies

- ❏ purple grapes
- ❏ green food coloring
- ❏ ice cube tray

Glowing Green Cocktail

ALCOHOLIC BEVERAGE

This creepy concoction emits an eerie glow when served with a plastic glow stick for a swizzle stick!

Directions

- Fill a glass with ice, pour in melon liqueur and rum, and fill the rest of the glass with pineapple juice and lemon-lime soda or ginger ale.
- Snap the glow stick to activate it, following package directions. Insert in glass and serve.

Hints & ideas

- Glow sticks can be purchased at many toy stores and novelty stores.

Party Favors & Crafts

A great idea for a children's Halloween party is to have the guests make crafts that they can take home. Children love to use their creative skills and will be proud to show off the creepy crafts they made. This section includes a variety of options for keeping the young (and young at heart) occupied at this fearsome and fun time of year! You can also have children make some of the crafts that are listed in the Indoor Decorations section: Glowing Jars (page 54), Halloween Paper Chains (page 47) or Hovering Bats (page 48).

Keep the ages of your guests in mind when planning the crafts. Young children, with supervision, can handle making some of the simpler crafts included in this section, while older children and adults might have fun making some of the more complex crafts. Also keep in mind the following tips:

- Keep small pieces and potentially dangerous tools (such as scissors) out of reach of very young children.

- Ensure that all glues, paints, pens and other materials are nontoxic and washable.

If you want to send children home after the party with goody bags, consider including healthy snacks or nonedible treats, because the children will already be getting plenty of candy on Halloween night. Try some of the following items, many of which can be purchased at novelty, toy or craft stores:

- plastic spider rings or other Halloween jewelry
- Halloween stickers or books
- orange, green and black beads along with some black string for making necklaces
- balls that look like eyeballs
- small bags of orange and green popcorn (available at candy stores or specialty popcorn outlets).

✔ Another fun craft activity is to provide a selection of candles and wax stickers in Halloween colors and designs. Children can decorate their own candles to take home with them.

Lollipop Crafts

Lollipop spiders and ghosts are easy for children to make. They also look great at place settings or on a buffet table.

Spooky Lollipop Spider

Directions

- Place the lollipop on top of the center of one pipe cleaner. Twist each end of the pipe cleaner over so that it wraps around the handle of the lollipop.
- Repeat with the remaining three pipe cleaners and then position them so that it looks as if there are eight legs.
- Bend the legs as shown in the picture.
- If you wish, cover the top of the lollipop with a small piece of black fabric and tie it on with black thread or string.
- Stick the craft eyes on top of the overlapped pipe cleaners. The knot of pipe cleaners will look like the spider's head and the lollipop its body.

Supplies

- ❑ 1 lollipop
- ❑ 4 black pipe cleaners
- ❑ small square of black fabric (optional)
- ❑ black thread or string (optional)
- ❑ small pair of stick-on craft eyes

114

Ghastly Lollipop Ghost

Directions

- From the white tissue paper or fabric, cut a square 8" × 8" (20 cm × 20 cm).
- Cut the ribbons into lengths of 6–8" (15–20 cm).
  - Put the lollipop in the center of the paper or fabric. Wrap the fabric over the lollipop to form a head.
- Tie the ribbons around the "neck" and make a bow.
- With a black marker, draw a face onto the head of each ghost (or use stick-on craft eyes).

Supplies

- ❑ 1 lollipop
- ❑ white tissue paper or thin fabric or felt
- ❑ narrow orange or black ribbon
- ❑ black marker or pair of stick-on craft eyes
- ❑ scissors

Hints & ideas

- If you choose to have children make these as a party activity, provide them with precut fabric squares and ribbons and have them draw their own faces on the ghosts.
- Red or black yarn can be used instead of ribbons.

Creepy Styrofoam Critters

These are terrific, simple crafts for little ghosts and goblins. In addition to the supplies listed, you will need a small paintbrush, scissors, toothpicks and white glue.

Wiggly Spider

Directions

- Paint the ball with black acrylic paint. Let dry.
- Cut the pipe cleaners into 3" (7.5 cm) pieces. Insert four pieces into each side of the spider to form eight legs. Bend the legs to form joints.
- Glue the eyes in place.
- To add a mouth, glue on a small piece of red felt cut in a mouth shape.

Supplies

- ☐ one 1½" (4 cm) Styrofoam ball
- ☐ black acrylic paint
- ☐ two 12" (30 cm) black pipe cleaners
- ☐ 1 pair of craft eyes
- ☐ 1 small piece of red felt (optional)

Crawling Ant

Directions

- Paint the Styrofoam balls with black acrylic paint. Let dry.
- Glue the balls together to form a row, or attach using toothpicks.
- Cut the pipe cleaners into six 3" (7.5 cm) lengths. Poke one piece into one side of the head and the other two pieces into the body to form the ant's legs. Repeat on the other side. Bend the legs to form joints.
- From the remaining pipe cleaner, cut two 1½–2" (4–5 cm) pieces for the ant's antennae. Glue a small pompom onto the top of each antenna.
- Poke the antennae into the top of the ant's head.
- Glue the eyes into place.

Supplies

- ☐ two 1½" (4 cm) Styrofoam balls
- ☐ black acrylic paint
- ☐ two 12" (30 cm) black pipe cleaners
- ☐ 1 pair of craft eyes
- ☐ 2 tiny red pompoms, about ¼" (6 mm) across

Caterpillar

Directions

- Paint the Styrofoam balls with green acrylic paint. Let dry.
- Cut the pipe cleaner into one 5" (13 cm) piece and two 1½" (4 cm) pieces.
- Use a toothpick to poke a hole through three of the Styrofoam balls. Slide the long piece of pipe cleaner through the balls, roughly centering the three balls in the length of the pipe cleaner.
- Apply glue to the ends of the pipe cleaner and then attach another Styrofoam ball to each end.
- Glue the eyes into place.
- Use the two smaller pieces of pipe cleaner for antennae. Insert them into the top of the head. Glue a small pompom onto the top of each antenna.
- If you like, add a felt mouth.

Supplies

- five 1½" (4 cm) Styrofoam balls
- green acrylic paint
- 1 thick green or black pipe cleaner, 8" (20 cm) long
- 1 pair of craft eyes
- 2 white or red pompons, about ¼" (6 mm) across
- red acrylic paint
- small piece of red felt (optional)

✔ To make it easier to paint the Styrofoam pieces, poke a toothpick into the piece and hold the toothpick while you are painting. You can then poke the other end of the toothpick into a sheet of Styrofoam to allow the pieces to dry without touching any surfaces.

✔ To attach pieces of Styrofoam to one another, use small pieces of toothpick. For added stability, dip each tip in glue before inserting into the pieces.

Pompom Critters

These soft and cuddly critters look a little more sinister when placed in unexpected spots. They are easy to put together with pompoms. Follow our suggestions for the size of the pompoms or use larger ones if you like.

Wriggly Caterpillar

Directions

- Glue the five black or green pompoms together to make the caterpillar's body. Let the glue dry (see Hints & Ideas).
- For each antenna, glue five red pompoms together. Let the glue dry and then glue the antenna to the caterpillar's head.
- Glue on the eyes.

Hints & ideas

- White glue or tacky craft glue works well with pompoms, but be

Supplies

- ❑ five 1–1½" (2.5–4 cm) pompoms, green or black
- ❑ ten ¼" (6 mm) red pompoms
- ❑ 1 pair small craft eyes
- ❑ white glue

Spider Softy

Directions

- Cut the pipe cleaners in half, creating four 6" (15 cm) lengths for the spider's legs. Twist the four pieces of pipe cleaner together, creating a center with four legs on either side. Flatten the center down a bit.

- Glue the larger black pompom onto the middle of the legs. Rearrange the pipe cleaner legs, bending them as you like.

- Glue the smaller black pompom on as a head.

- For the eyes, glue on craft eyes or two small red pompoms.

Supplies

- ❑ one 1–1½" (2.5–4 cm) black pompom
- ❑ one ½" (13 mm) black pompom
- ❑ two 12" (30 cm) black pipe cleaners
- ❑ two ¼" (6 mm) red pompoms or 1 pair small craft eyes
- ❑ white glue

Freaky Eyeballs

Creating eyeballs from Styrofoam balls will keep young party guests busy, and they will love taking this unique craft home with them.

Directions

- In pencil, sketch an eye onto each ball by tracing around a dime or other round object.
- Color the pupils black and the irises blue or brown. Then use the red pen to draw veins extending back through the eyeball.

Hints & ideas

- Some novelty stores sell balls that already look like eyeballs. You may wish to purchase a couple of these as models to work from.
- Ping-Pong balls can be used instead of Styrofoam balls.

Supplies

- ❑ small Styrofoam balls
- ❑ fine-tip permanent markers in black, blue, brown
- ❑ extra-fine-tip permanent marker in red
- ❑ dimes (or other small round objects)
- ❑ pencil

Pumpkin Seed Jewelry

Save your pumpkin seeds and let older children thread them onto strings to make great Halloween necklaces and bracelets. These strands also make good decorations.

Directions

- Thread the needle and knot the thread at one end.
- Thread the seeds on one at a time, pushing the needle through at the center of each seed.
- If you wish, you can thread on some beads intermittently to provide your jewelry with some added color.
- Candy corn lends a nice touch to the jewelry as well (see photo), but the candy is prone to break when you push the needle through it. To keep the candy from breaking, warm the needle slightly over a flame just before pushing it through the candy corn. Ensure adult supervision of this step.

Hints & ideas

- Pumpkin seeds, especially if they are roasted, can be quite tough to push a needle through. Use a large needle and, if necessary, pull the needle through by grabbing it with small pliers.
- Strings of pumpkin seeds look great as decorative accents. Try placing a strand around the base of an orange or black candle or twisting a long strand through your table centerpiece.

Supplies

- ❏ pumpkin seeds
- ❏ orange, black and green beads (optional)
- ❏ decorations for your jewelry (optional)
- ❏ large embroidery or craft needle
- ❏ cotton thread

Magnificent Magnets

These Halloween magnets make a great craft activity at a party or serve as unique party favors. Children will be delighted to display them on their fridges at home.

Supplies

- ☐ sheets of craft foam in various colors
- ☐ magnetic tape (or strips of magnet and glue)
- ☐ markers: black, silver
- ☐ pencil
- ☐ scissors

Directions

- Draw a design on a piece of craft foam. Follow our examples or create a pattern of your own. Cut the piece out; this will form the base of your magnet.
- Draw any accent features you want (eyes, noses, etc.) onto appropriately colored sheets of craft foam.
- Carefully cut out the shapes and then use markers to decorate them.
- Glue the accent pieces onto the base piece.
- Cut the magnetic tape or strip of magnet into pieces that are approximately 1" × 1" (2.5 cm × 2.5 cm).
- Peel off the back of the magnetic strip and attach it to the foam shape; use glue to attach the magnet if you do not have magnetic tape.

Hints & ideas

Use a hole punch to cut circles out of craft foam, perfect for eyes on the magnets.

Some ideas for magnets: ghost (white foam and black marker), tombstone (white or gray foam and black marker), jack-o'-lantern (orange foam and black marker), witch's face (green foam and black marker), black cat (black foam and silver marker) or bat (black foam and silver marker).

Petrifying Paddleballs

Decorate these paddleballs yourself and give them out as party favors, or paint the base color and then have children add their own designs. Try some of the patterns shown or come up with your own!

Supplies

- ☐ acrylic paint sealer
- ☐ acrylic paints: black, orange, white, gray or silver, yellow, red
- ☐ paddleballs (purchased from toy or craft stores)
- ☐ tracing paper
- ☐ paintbrushes

Directions

- Seal the paddles, both top and bottom, with acrylic paint sealer.
- Trace a pattern or come up with an idea of your own. See our photos and the Hints & Ideas section opposite for some pattern suggestions.
- Paint the top side of the paddle in the background color of your choice. Let dry.
- Using transfer paper, transfer your pattern to the painted side of the paddleball. Paint features with acrylic paint. Let dry, then seal with acrylic paint sealer.
- You can also draw designs on the ball. Make it into a miniature jack-o'-lantern or add a couple of tiny black bats, for example.

Hints & ideas

Here are some ideas for patterns:

- **Jack-o'-Lantern** Paint the paddle orange and add accents with black and yellow paint. You can paint the handle green for the pumpkin's stem.
- **Bats Under a Full Moon** Paint the paddle gray or silver and add black bats and a yellow moon. For spooky bat eyes, dip the tip of a pencil eraser in white or yellow paint and dab on. Use a marker to draw in the pupils.
- **Black Cat and Flying Witch** Paint the paddle silver or orange and add a cat and a flying witch with black paint. Paint the cat's eyes yellow.
- **Ghost** Paint the paddle white and add a spooky or a friendly ghost face with black paint. Use your imagination and add extra touches such as an orange and black bow tie around the handle.
- **Ghoul or Monster** Paint the paddle green or gray. Add a scary face and a scar or two.
- **Vampire** Paint the paddle white or light gray (mix white and darker gray paint). Add black hair in a widow's peak, black eyebrows and features, and yellow fangs (or draw them with a black marker). Use red droplets of paint to suggest blood dripping from the vampire's mouth. Paint the handle black as part of the cape.

Witch's Hand Full of Treats

A glove filled with popcorn makes a perfect take-home treat.

Directions

- Fill the glove with popcorn.
- Tie the yarn or ribbon around the end of the glove to keep it closed.
- Add a spider ring to one of the fingers and plastic fingernails on each finger.

Variation

- Insert a piece of candy corn, pointy side down, into each fingertip of the glove to resemble the witch's fingernails.

Hints & ideas

- Look for colored popcorn at candy stores or popcorn outlets.

Slithering Slime

Directions

- In one bowl, mix ½ cup (125 ml) water with 1 cup (250 ml) glue and a few drops of green food coloring.
- In another bowl, stir the borax into the remaining ½ cup (125 ml) water.
- Slowly add the borax mixture into the green glue mixture. Stir the combination until it becomes as slimy as you like. To increase the sliminess, add a bit more water.
- If the mixture becomes hard, that is an indication that too much of the borax mixture was added. Add a bit of water or begin a new mixture.
- Slime can be stored in the fridge in resealable bags or tightly sealed jars for about 10 days.

Variation

- For a simpler slime, pour 1 cup (250 ml) cornstarch into a bowl. To the cornstarch add 8–9 tbsp. (120–135 ml) water, one spoon at a time. Mix in a few drops of food coloring. Continue to mix until you have a smooth mixture.
- The cornstarch will naturally settle on the bottom of your container, but you just have to keep mixing (using your hands is the best method) and it will become smooth and slimy again. This mixture keeps in a covered container in the fridge for about 10 days.

Menacing Masks

Children will love transforming paper plates into frightful faces.

Directions

- Hold a paper plate up to your face to determine the proper locations for the features.
- Choose a design for your mask (see our list) and draw a face on the plate. Carefully cut out the features, using a utility knife for the eyes and other interior cuts.
- Once you have cut out the features, decorate the mask if you desire. Use colored markers or paint, glitter glue, sequins, beads and whatever else you can come up with! If you wish, glue or tape on some crepe paper, yarn or feathers for hair.
- For added emphasis, you can outline features with a black or green marker. Dab on some paint for moles, spots, whiskers, stitches and so on.
- Measure a piece of elasticized string to fit around your head. Staple it at each side of the mask, and knot the ends to secure it.

Supplies

- ❑ paper plates, either white or in Halloween colors (black, orange, green, purple, white, silver)
- ❑ paints: orange, black, green, metallic, etc. (optional)
- ❑ markers: black, green, gray, white, etc. (optional)
- ❑ decorative touches such as glitter, sequins, beads, feathers, curling ribbon, crepe paper, yarn, pipe cleaners (optional)
- ❑ elasticized string
- ❑ pencil
- ❑ scissors
- ❑ utility knife
- ❑ stapler

Hints & ideas

- If you are not able to purchase colored paper plates, use white paper plates. Leave them white or paint them the color you want and let them dry before decorating them.

Mask ideas

- **Jack-o'-Lantern** Use an orange paper plate. Cut out eyes, a nose and a mouth. Also, trim off the top of the plate, leaving a piece for the stem. You can paint or color the stem brown or green; consider outlining the facial features with black marker or glitter glue.

- **Pirate** Use a white or green mask. Cut out a hat from construction paper. Cut out one eye, a crooked nose and a mouth with only a couple of teeth. Color or paint a patch over one eye, blacken the teeth and add some scars. Add a construction paper hat or staple a crepe paper scarf to the top of the mask.
- **Skeleton** Use a white paper plate. Cut out spooky eyes and a nose, and use a black marker to draw the teeth.
- **Cat** Use a white or black paper plate. Cut out ears from the top, slanted cat eyes and a small nose. Staple on some pipe cleaner whiskers, or draw or paint them in gray or white. You may wish to glue on some black feathers or yarn as fur.
- **Masquerade-Style Variation** You can make smaller masks that are held up with a wooden stick or even a plastic straw to cover the eyes. If such a mask is worn as part of a costume, apply makeup to the parts of the face that won't be covered by the mask.
- **BOO!** A simple masquerade-style mask can be made by cutting out two Os for the eyes, adding a B in front of them and an exclamation mark after them, and outlining the Os with a black marker. Add decorative touches with metallic markers or glitter pens.

Grim Miniature Graveyard

This makes a wonderful decoration, and you can involve young party guests in constructing it.

Directions

- With a sharp knife, cut the Styrofoam piece in half across the longest side. One of these pieces will become the graveyard.

- Measure the other Styrofoam piece into four tombstone shapes, each about 3" (7.5 cm) wide. Mark the divisions with a pencil or pen and a ruler.

- Cut out the tombstones, trimming them so that their edges are as smooth as possible. You may wish to round off the tops of a couple of them so that they are not all the same size and shape.

- Insert two toothpicks into the bottom of each tombstone and then fasten each tombstone to the graveyard piece. Allow for some space between the tombstones.

- Set the display on some newspaper. Paint the graveyard and tombstones with a light coat of paint, either spraying if using spray paint or brushing or sponging paint on. You do not have to be careful to paint the middle of the graveyard, as that will be covered by the Spanish moss. Let the paint dry.

- Glue Spanish moss on the base of the graveyard. Drape some on the tombstones too if you like.

Supplies

- 1 sheet of Styrofoam, approximately 24" × 32" × 1" (60 cm × 80 cm × 2.5 cm)
- toothpicks
- newspaper
- dark gray acrylic paint (see Hints & Ideas)
- fine-tip black marker
- Spanish moss
- 2–3 small plastic bugs
- small twigs
- flat stones
- sharp knife (such as a paring or utility knife)
- pencil or pen
- ruler
- paintbrush (optional)

- Create a stepping stone path by gluing flat rocks among the tombstones.
- Decorate the graveyard by adding some small plastic bugs and pieces of dry twigs or vine.
- If you want to create a twig fence, cut the twigs at an angle on one end and push that end through the Styrofoam. Secure the twigs by taping the underside of the graveyard, where the twigs poke through. Build a fence by attaching the twigs together, either with glue or, for a more natural look, small pieces of hemp thread.

Hints & ideas

- If you are having children assemble this craft, paint and cut the Styrofoam graveyard and tombstones a day in advance.
- The paint must be acrylic. Other paint will cause the foam to disintegrate.
- You can use any size of Styrofoam sheet for this craft.

Ghoulish Games

Ghosts and goblins of all ages will enjoy getting into the spirit of things with a few Halloween games and activities. You'll find ideas in this section for young creepy creatures as well as the (supposedly) more mature variety, and you can adapt many of these games to suit different age groups.

Games are particularly popular with younger party guests, especially if the host offers small prizes and rewards. Check the Party Favors & Crafts section for some simple prize ideas, or visit your local novelty or dollar store for inexpensive goodies to pass out.

At a Halloween party for adults, try to anticipate what your guests are interested in doing. Sometimes the most important thing a party host can do is set a spooky scene. When you have an assortment of gruesome decorations, eerie music in the background, scary movies playing, a frightful concoction of food and drinks and a group of costumed people determined to enjoy themselves—that's often all you need for a successful monster bash. (For scary music and movie suggestions, see page 15.) Many of these games are so much fun, though, that your guests are bound to want to get involved.

Crazy Costume Contest

Supplies

☐ novelty trophies or Halloween-themed prizes

Announce a costume contest and let your party guests pick the winners! Give out small prizes in categories such as Best Overall, Scariest, Ugliest, Funniest, Cutest, Best Homemade, Not Sure What It Is, Most Unique, Most Colorful and Least Amount of Effort.

Ages: preschool to adult

Directions

- Inform your guests that you are going to have a costume contest, and advise them of the different prize categories.
- Count the votes (verbally or by secret ballot) to see who wins in each category.
- Award the prizes and have a lot of laughs.

Hints & ideas

- When you hold a costume contest at a children's party, ensure that you have the same number of prize categories as guests. This way, every child gets a prize.

Balloon Relay

Teamwork is especially important in this relay, in which pairs of contestants race to place balloons into baskets without using their hands.

Ages: kids of all ages

Directions

- In a large area, set up the relay course. Use masking tape to mark off a start/finish line and set a row of laundry baskets at the other end of the course. Make sure that each team will have room to maneuver.
- Insert three inflated balloons into each garbage bag and instruct each pair of contestants to stand next to one of these bags.
- The two partners should stand back-to-back and balance one balloon between them. They must not use their hands while they transport each balloon to the laundry basket, and if they drop a balloon, they must return to the start line and start over.
- On your signal, the teams get one balloon at a time out of the garbage bag, race to drop a balloon into a laundry basket, then run back to the start/finish line and repeat the process until all three balloons are in the basket. The pair that gets their balloons in their basket first wins.
- Award the winning team a prize.

Hints & ideas

- To make the game more difficult for older guests, have them blow up the balloons themselves before doing the back-to-back race.

Pumpkin Pageantry Contest

A simple and festive way to keep guests busy is to have them roll up their sleeves and decorate an assortment of pumpkins.

Ages: preschool to adult

Directions

- Line a table with newspaper to make cleanup easier.
- Inform guests of the award categories and provide them with the necessary supplies and tools.
- Instruct the participants to use their imaginations and create a variety of pumpkin masterpieces.
- Have the entire group vote on the winner in each category. Ensure that for younger children, you have as many categories as you do guests so that each guest will be a winner.

Hints & ideas

- Some examples of categories might be Scariest, Funniest, Friendliest, Most Unique, Most Colorful and Most Bizarre.

Adult variation

- You can modify this contest to involve jack-o'-lantern carving. Provide guests with larger pumpkins, carving tools, design templates, pencils, markers and decorative accents. See page 70 for pumpkin-carving ideas.

Supplies

- ❑ pumpkins of various sizes—large, small or ornamental
- ❑ colored and metallic markers
- ❑ glitter pens
- ❑ stickers
- ❑ small decorative touches (sequins, pieces of felt, etc.)
- ❑ glue
- ❑ scissors

Dr. Frankenstein's Laboratory

are your guests to plunge
eir hands into bowls filled
th mysterious and disgusting
pecimens."

rections

n a dim room, set up a row of bowls
along a table. It is best to blindfold
your guests so that they cannot see
he contents of the bowls they are
sticking their hands into.

In a creepy voice, tell your guests
hat they are about to visit Dr.
Frankenstein's laboratory, and that
hey will touch some of his
specimens and ingredients.

Lead your guests one at a time along
he row of specimens, instructing
hem to touch the contents of each
bowl. As they reach into each one, tell
hem what they are touching; e.g.,
'eyeballs" for a bowl of peeled grapes.

ints & ideas

Have some eerie music playing in the
background to intensify the experience.

Another terrifying item to include is an artificial skull, if you are
able to purchase or borrow one.

If you would rather not blindfold your guests, you can place the
tems in labeled jars. Try to cover the outsides of the jars with the
abels so that it is less likely that guests will be able to see the
actual contents. Dim the lights slightly and let the guests feel thei
way along the specimen table. Another alternative is to cut hand-
sized holes in the tops of boxes and place the bowls inside them

Supplies

- ❑ cooked spaghetti (intestines)
- ❑ peeled grapes (eyeballs)
- ❑ chunk of gelatin (liver, heart)
- ❑ small, damp carrots (fingers)
- ❑ cracked nutshells (toenails)
- ❑ overcooked cauliflower (brains)
- ❑ piece of hot dog (nose)
- ❑ dried pears or apricots (ears)
- ❑ small pieces of chalk or corn kernels (teeth)
- ❑ rubber glove full of crushed ice (corpse's hand)
- ❑ wig or corn silk (corpse's hair)
- ❑ several bowls
- ❑ blindfold

Flying Witch Relay

Have your guests run a race without losing their brooms and witches' hats!

Ages: children

Directions

- In a large area where guests can safely race, set up a finish line. For example, have guests run to a wall, touch it and then race back to the starting point.
- If you wish, you can mark the finish line with a piece of string or a line of masking tape.
- Supply each contestant with a witch hat and a broom. Inform them that their hat must remain on and they must continue to "ride" the broom throughout the race; otherwise, they will have to start over.
- On your signal, have the witches "fly" through the race, awarding a prize to the first witch to return to the finish line with both hat and broom intact.

Hints & ideas

- If you have many guests, you can do this relay in heats and have the winners of each heat face off in a final race.

Supplies

- ❑ witch hats—1 for each participant
- ❑ brooms—1 for each participant
- ❑ masking tape or string

138

Encase the Mummy

See how fast your team can cover a mummy with a continuous wrapping of toilet paper! This game tests dexterity and teamwork.

Ages: first grade to adult

Directions

- Divide your party guests into teams. Each team must select one member to be their "mummy." The remaining team members will wrap the mummy.
- Provide each team with two rolls of toilet paper, one roll of tape and a garbage bag.
- Tell the teams that they must wrap their mummy from head to toe, except for the mummy's nose and mouth. No skin or clothing can remain visible through the wrappings.
- Explain that if the mummy's wrapping breaks or tears, the team must repair it with tape.
- On your signal, the teams may begin. The team that finishes first wins the game, provided that their mummy is completely covered.

Supplies

Each team will require
- ☐ 2 rolls of toilet paper
- ☐ 1 roll of clear adhesive tape
- ☐ 1 garbage bag

Hints & ideas

- Provide some incentive for the mummy-wrappers to help clean up the mess afterwards. Suggest that the team that unwraps its mummy the fastest, stuffing all of the wrap in the garbage bag, also wins a prize.

Wacky Pumpkin Bowling

Supplies
- ❏ small round pumpkins with stems removed or foam balls that resemble pumpkins
- ❏ plastic bowling pins
- ❏ masking tape

This game is great fun for children and adults alike, especially when a real pumpkin is used as a wobbly, unpredictable bowling ball!

Ages: preschool to adult

Directions
- In a large area, set up a bowling lane with plastic pins at the end. Mark a lane with masking tape to indicate where the ball should be rolled.
- Depending on the number of guests playing, you might want to divide them into bowling teams.
- Explain the object of the game, provide teams with small pumpkins or balls and let the games begin.

Hints & ideas
- You might want to allow your guests three turns and let them keep their best score.
- If you do not have plastic bowling pins (available at most toy stores), use plastic soft drink bottles half-filled with water and sealed tightly.

The Apple Grab

Supplies

☐ string, enough for a piece 3–4' (1–1.2 m) long for each guest
☐ small apples, enough for 1 per guest
☐ clothesline or heavy rope to suspend the apples from
☐ scissors
☐ large needle

This game looks much easier than it is. Watching party guests race to take the first bite from a dangling apple makes for a lot of laughs.

Ages: first grade to adult

Directions

- Cut string into 3–4' (1–1.2 m) lengths according to the number of guests. The length of string depends on the height of the guests and whether you are suspending the strings from the ceiling or from a clothesline.
- With a large needle and starting at the top of each apple and threading down through the core, thread each piece of string through one side of an apple core and then back through the other side of the core. Tie a knot in the string. (Alternatively, if the apples' stems seem to be secure, you can tie the string to them.)
- Hang a clothesline or rope across the room.
- Tie the apples' strings to the clothesline, varying the heights in case some guests are taller than others.
- Have each guest stand by an apple that reaches him/her at shoulder height. Adjust the length of the string if necessary.
- Explain the object of the game and tell guests that they cannot use their hands, elbows or shoulders to help them position the apples.
- On your signal, the guests try to take bites from their apples. The game ends when someone succeeds.

Pin the Mouth on the Pumpkin

Supplies

- ❏ 1 sheet of orange poster board
- ❏ black construction paper
- ❏ black marker
- ❏ white crayons or gel pens
- ❏ scissors
- ❏ glue
- ❏ tape
- ❏ blindfold

Young partygoers (and those who are young at heart) will love this version of the ever-popular Pin the Tail on the Donkey game!

Ages: preschool to third grade

Directions

- Draw a large pumpkin on the orange poster board. Cut it out.
- Draw two eyes and a nose on the black construction paper. Cut them out.
- Glue the eyes and nose to the poster board and tape the pumpkin to the wall.
- Cut several mouths from the piece of black construction paper (one per child).
- Have the children write their names on the mouths, using white crayons or gel pens that are visible on black.
- Attach a piece of tape to the back of each pumpkin mouth.
- Explain that the children must stick their pumpkin mouths to the first spot they touch when they reach the pumpkin.
- Blindfold the children one at a time, spin them around once and tell them when to go.
- Once all the children have had a turn, check to see which child's pumpkin mouth is in the best position, and award a prize.

Hints & ideas

- Other versions to try: Pin the Tail on the Black Cat, Pin the Hat on the Wicked Witch, Pin the Mouth on the Ghost, etc.

Find the Bones Rac

A challenging searching game is a great way to get your guests working together and having fun.

Ages: fourth grade to adult

Directions

- Ahead of time, take the skeletons apart. Hide all the parts around the room. (See Hints & Ideas for some tips about hiding the parts.)
- Divide the participants into teams of two or three each. Each team must search the room to find the parts of the skeleton and then reassemble the skeleton.
- If teams are searching at the same time, the winning team is the one that assembles its skeleton first. An alternative is to let teams take turns searching for the skeleton parts while you time their efforts. The winning team then is the one that reassembles the skeleton in the shortest time.

Hints & ideas

- The skeletons could look slightly different, with different background colors, for example, so that the teams are less likely to get the parts mixed up. To keep things fair, make sure all the skeletons have an equal number of parts.
- To make the search a little easier, divide the room into sections and hide each team's skeleton in only one section of the room.
- Using glow-in-the-dark skeletons in a darkened room would add another spooky and challenging aspect to this game.

Supplies

- ❑ purchased plastic hard cardboard skeletons, one for team

Sinister Scavenger Hunt

Supplies
- ☐ paper
- ☐ pencils
- ☐ garbage bags or other containers

Your guests will have a riot searching frantically for items in this Halloween scavenger hunt.

Ages: second grade to adult

Directions

- Write the words HAPPY HALLOWEEN, or some other phrase, vertically down the left-hand side of each team's piece of paper. Strike out the second occurrence of any repeating letters so that no letters appear on the vertical list more than once.
- Divide your guests into teams and give each team a scavenger hunt list, a pencil and a bag or container.
- Explain the game to the participants. The team to find the most objects that begin with the letters on the list wins.
- As they find an item corresponding to a certain letter, the players write the name of the object on their list and put it into the bag or container. Give them 10–15 minutes to find as many items as they can. Each team should find no more than one object for each letter.
- On your signal, instruct the teams to begin to search the room, floor or house.
- When the time is up, have the teams sit in their groups. As you call out each of the letters on the list, each team is to hold up their corresponding object. Each team gets a point for each letter they were able to match with an object.

Hints & ideas

- Adult teams can be sent on a neighborhood-wide scavenger hunt, searching for specific items that you come up with on a detailed list.
- Alter the phrase to be whatever you want.
- For younger children especially, ensure that there are items around for them to find so they can feel successful about the hunt.

More Hilarious Halloween Activities

Modify old favorites to incorporate the Halloween theme. For example, a Halloween candy or toy hunt could be set up like an Easter egg hunt. Be inventive and don't be afraid to modify games to suit your guests' ages or interests.

Crazy Pumpkin Pass

Have your awkward, costume-clad guests pass around a small or ornamental pumpkin (with the stem removed) without using their hands! Start by placing the pumpkin under someone's chin and watch as the pumpkin takes a wacky route from person to person. A variation including music could be to have all participants sit in a circle and pass a Halloween item around while music is playing (Halloween music, of course). Whoever is holding the object when the music stops is out. The last person remaining at the end of the game is the winner.

Eerie Fortune-Teller

Ask an imaginative friend—someone your guests don't know—to dress up as a mysterious fortune-teller. (Of course, you can also hire an actual fortune-teller; this would be a big hit at a party for adults or teens.) Have her wear colorful clothes and scarves, a kerchief around her head and lots of jewelry, and instruct her to speak in a slow, spooky voice. In a small, candlelit room, set up a table with a crystal ball (you can use a small ball with a scarf draped overtop). One by one, your guests can enter the room and ask the fortune-teller questions. She can be as spooky or as funny as she wants—as long as she doesn't say anything really negative. You may want to secretly tell the fortune-teller a little about the guests before they take their turns.

Ghastly Ghost Stories

A great way to set a haunting Halloween mood is to tell a chilling ghost story. Make sure you choose stories that are age appropriate and will not frighten any children in attendance. Have your guests sit in a circle in a darkened room, with only a flashlight or candle for light. Make your story personal if possible, and even have it take place in your house ("In this very house, many years ago, there lived an evil old witch…"). For a collection of chilling stories, look for Ghost House Books' *Campfire Ghost Stories* and *Haunted Halloween Stories* (see ordering information on last page of book).

Draw-the-word Game

In a plastic Halloween pail or other container, place several slips of paper with Halloween words written on them (e.g., jack-o'-lantern, witch, bat, spooky, spider, candy, costume, pumpkin, vampire, mummy, ghoul, monster, ghost). You will need a chalkboard or a large pad of paper on an easel. Divide your guests into two teams. A player from the first team begins by picking out one slip of paper and then drawing pictures related to the word. That person's team tries to guess the word within a one- or two-minute time limit. The other team goes next, and you keep alternating until everyone has had a chance to draw. The team that has the most correct guesses wins.

Chilling Charades

Older children and adults often love to play charades. Have teams act out phrases from popular scary movies and books. Consult the lists on page 15 of this book and use your imagination to come up with some terrifically spooky phrases and words!

Creepy Costumes & Menacing Makeup

Transforming yourself into a witch, ghoul, scarecrow, monster or other creature is one of the most exciting aspects of Halloween. There are hundreds of costumes on the market, and they range from simple and inexpensively made to complex and worth hundreds of dollars. It is also relatively easy to create your own costumes, often from materials and supplies that you already have on hand. Making a Halloween costume doesn't have to take a lot of time or cost a fortune, and you can get some excellent effects with everyday items and imaginative makeup application.

Costume Hints & Ideas

- For inexpensive clothing and accessories, try Goodwill stores, thrift shops, consignment stores, dollar stores, etc.

- You are most likely using your costume for only one night, so it need not be elaborate or well constructed. Gluing or stapling can often substitute for sewing.

- Many of these costumes and accessories are also useful for other costume occasions such as theme parties or plays. Use your imagination to modify any costume to make it suit your taste, needs and budget.

- For easy-to-make paper plate masks, check out the Menacing Masks craft on page 128.

Tips for Children's Costumes

- Make or purchase costumes that are comfortable enough for children to wear for several hours.

- Costumes should be lightweight and fit properly yet large enough that warm clothing can be worn underneath if it's a chilly evening for trick-or-treating.

- Ensure that the costumes are not too bulky, so that children can easily walk without tripping or entangling their feet.

- Children should wear comfortable shoes to avoid sore feet, falls and spilled treat pails.

- Makeup is recommended because it is more comfortable than a mask and does not obscure vision, as a mask might. If your child must wear a mask, it should have openings for the nose and mouth and large eyeholes to allow for full vision.

- Wigs, hats, beards and whiskers should be fastened securely and should not obscure vision.

- Ensure that children are easily visible at night by using light colors and adding reflective tape, available at hardware or sporting goods stores, to costumes.

- Buy flame-resistant costumes or make them from flame-resistant fabric.

- Knives, swords, magic wands and other such props must be harmless and made from cardboard or a pliable material that will not cause anyone injury. Never allow children to carry real weapons or other sharp objects.

- Treat bags or pails should be light in color or trimmed with reflective tape. It is wise to have children carry a flashlight to ensure that they can see and be seen easily when trick-or-treating.

Easy-to-make Costumes

Black cat

Wear black tights or pants, a black sweater or turtleneck and black shoes. Add a black tail and a hood with ears (or a black headband with ears sewn onto it). For makeup, apply black whiskers, a cat nose and a pink mouth.

Devil

Wear red tights or pants and a red turtleneck or sweater. Wear large red socks over your shoes or boots and a red hood or headband with horns sewn on. Add a red tail and gloves, and carry a pitchfork (use a broom handle with a painted cardboard fork). Apply red makeup, black eyebrows, lined eyes and a black mustache and goatee.

Diver

If you have access to a wetsuit, wear it along with a mask, snorkel and flippers. Slick your hair back with hair gel so that it looks wet, and carry a pail with some water and plastic fish in it.

152

Dracula

The most fun part of this costume is wearing plastic fangs! Put on a white dress shirt, dark pants, dark shoes and socks, a dark bow tie, a black opera cape and a long scarf (preferably red). Slick your hair back with gel and use makeup to create a black widow's peak on your forehead near the hairline. Cover your face and neck with white makeup and add dark hollows and lines on your face, vampire eyes, bushy black eyebrows and dark lips. You can use makeup to make it look as if a few drops of blood are dripping from your mouth.

Gypsy

This one is easy if you have a puffy blouse, a long flowered skirt and a scarf to wear over your hair. Add an embroidered shawl (raid your grandma's closet!) and gold hoop earrings, and wear lots of makeup. Don't forget the blue eye shadow!

Mummy

Using hair gel, slick your hair back and away from your face. Apply white face makeup with dark eye sockets, and add a couple of scars if you wish. Wrap strips of elastic bandage or muslin around your entire body, making sure to leave joints so that you can bend your arms and legs. It works well to attach the strips of muslin to white or cream-colored thermal underwear. Pin or lightly stitch the strips in place. To make the muslin look old and worn, dip pieces in tea and allow to dry.

Nerd

Wear polyester clothes and mismatched patterns. Pull your pants up high so that they look too short, and wear a tight shirt with a wide collar, a bow tie and white socks with black shoes. Wrap some masking tape around the center of a pair of dark-framed glasses and slick your hair back with gel. Add a pocket protector with a few pens in it.

Pirate

Roll up a pair of jeans or dark pants to just below the knee, and add tights or knee socks, dark boots or shoes (with large buckles if possible), a large puffy shirt, a sash or belt, an eye patch (or makeup to resemble one), a bandanna, a vest and one gold earring. Makeup should consist of heavy eyebrows, a curling mustache, scars and even a skull and crossbones tattoo. Carry a cardboard or plastic hook and dagger.

Robot

Use a cardboard box with holes for your arms and legs, and a smaller box for the robot's head. Glue aluminum foil pie plates to the front as robot components, and use glow sticks for antennae. Decorate the boxes with silver spray paint or aluminum foil. If your face is visible, wear silver or green makeup.

Costumes

Scarecrow

Add patches to old jeans and a long-sleeved flannel shirt, and use duct tape to attach some straw to the inside cuffs of shirt and pants. If you wish, stuff the shirt to create a stuffed scarecrow look. Wear a straw hat, paint on rosy cheeks and red lips and carry a broom.

Sherlock Holmes

Wear a brown cape, a vest, white pants and a deerstalker hat. Carry a magnifying glass and pretend to be looking for clues.

Skeleton

Create bones with strips of white tape on a black leotard or turtleneck and tights. Wear white or gray face makeup with blackened, ghoulish eyes.

Spider

Wear a black leotard and tights, or a black turtleneck and pants. Stuff three or four pairs of black pantyhose with more black pantyhose to form the spider's legs. Pin or sew the legs to the waist of your leotard or pants. Wear a closely fitting cap and add black pipe cleaners for antennae. Makeup should be black or green.

Television

Cut a square hole out of the front of a cardboard box. Cover the hole with a thin colored transparent sheet (known as a gel) or piece of cellophane. Attach suspenders to the cardboard box so you can wear it. Hold or secure a flashlight inside the box so that the TV appears to be glowing. Use glow sticks or silver pipe cleaners for antennae.

Tourist

Wear a colorful floral shirt, shorts, sandals and socks, and a tacky hat. Wear one or two old cameras around your neck, sunglasses and zinc oxide on your nose. Tuck a map in one pocket.

The walking dead

For a ghoulish costume, wear dark pants or jeans streaked with mud, a ratty old shirt, beat-up shoes and wrinkled socks. Wear gray face makeup and add dark eye sockets, lips and nostrils. Draw scars on your face and hands.

Witch

What would Halloween be without some witches? Wear a black or dark skirt, a shapeless black/dark top, black shoes and tights (striped tights are a great touch), a short black cape and a witch's hat. Wear green face makeup, a fake nose, heavy black eyebrows, black lips, stringy hair (or a wig) and a blackened tooth. You can also purchase long fake nails or witch's hands, and carry a dirtied broom.

Last-minute Costumes

Bag of grapes
- top a black leotard or turtleneck and tights or pants with a clear garbage bag filled with green or purple balloons

Baseball/football/hockey/basketball player
- your own uniform and sports equipment

Cowboy/cowgirl
- jeans, western shirt, cowboy boots and hat, bandanna, belt with big buckle

Cruella De Vil (from *101 Dalmatians*)
- black and white wig, dark dress, dark tights, long gloves, boa or fake fur stole

Hobo
- large men's pants, old dark sports coat, shirt with patches, stick with a bandanna tied to it, dirtied face

Old man/woman
- old-looking clothes, reading glasses, old shoes, a bulky purse or old man's hat and a cane; add talcum powder to hair to make it look gray

1950s bebop look
- untucked, solid-color, button-down shirt; jeans rolled to mid-calf; socks and penny loafers; ponytail or slicked-back hair

1960s hippie
- bell-bottoms, tie-dyed shirt, Afro wig, sandals, love beads

1970s dude
- polyester pantsuit, vest, high-heeled boots or shoes, gaudy jewelry

More Simple Costumes
Accident-prone kid
Angel
Baby
Belly Dancer
Bride
Bumblebee
Bunny
Butterfly
Cheerleader
Clown
Doctor
Ghost
Gift box
Jailbird
Ladybug
Monster
Mouse
Nurse
Pumpkin

Horrid Hands

These frightening hands can be used as part of a costume or can be set up in your house as a Halloween decoration!

Supplies

- ❏ loose-fitting rubber gloves
- ❏ crumpled newspaper
- ❏ black marker
- ❏ strips of gauze bandage
- ❏ glue
- ❏ red paint or fake blood
- ❏ talcum powder

Directions

- Stuff the gloves with newspaper to make them easier to work with.
- With a black marker, color in the fingernails.
- Beginning with the fingers, wrap gauze strips around the entire gloves until they are completely bandaged.
- Glue the gauze down to prevent it from unraveling.
- Add some red "blood" to the hands.
- Before wearing the gloves, remove the newspaper and sprinkle talcum powder into the gloves so that they won't stick to your hands.

Makeup Tips

It is a good idea to wear makeup instead of a mask. Makeup is less expensive, safer for trick-or-treating, doesn't restrict movement or vision and can provide fantastic effects!

- You can purchase kits of Halloween makeup or theatrical greasepaint for great color and ease of application. Choose makeup that is labeled "Laboratory Tested," "Nontoxic" or "Meets Federal Standards for Cosmetics." Most brands list the ingredients and/or a chemical analysis on the package. Follow the manufacturer's instructions for application and removal.

- It is not essential to purchase Halloween makeup. Try the recipes on the next page or use eyeliner pencils, blush, eye shadows, lip liners, brow pencils, lipstick and flesh-colored makeup.

- Adults should supervise the application of makeup for young children. Keep makeup out of eyes.

- You will find a small jar of cold cream helpful for applying and removing makeup. Apply your makeup on top of a cold-cream base. Use cold cream and facial tissues to wipe it off, and wash with soap and warm water to remove any last traces.

Makeup Recipes

Face Makeup

It's easy and inexpensive to make your own makeup and customize the colors. The following recipe makes a small quantity of makeup that you can color as you need.

Supplies
- ❑ 1 tsp. (5 ml) cornstarch
- ❑ ½ tsp. (2.5 ml) cold cream
- ❑ ½ tsp. (2.5 ml) water
- ❑ food coloring

Directions

- In a small container, stir together the cold cream and cornstarch until the mixture is well blended. Add water and stir, then add the food coloring to make the color of makeup you need. Store the makeup in an airtight container.
- To apply, wash your face and dry thoroughly.
- Use fingertips to spread the makeup onto large areas of your face.
- Use a small paintbrush to paint designs on face.
- This makeup can be removed with soap and water.

Frightening Fake Blood

This fake blood looks surprisingly real! It may temporarily stain skin, and it will permanently stain most fabrics.

Supplies
- ❑ 1¾ cups (435 ml) corn syrup
- ❑ ¼ cup (60 ml) water
- ❑ 2 tsp. (10 ml) red food coloring
- ❑ 8–10 drops blue food coloring
- ❑ ¼ cup (60 ml) cornstarch, sifted

Directions

- In a container that seals tightly, mix corn syrup and water. Add both colors of food coloring, cover the container and shake well.
- Add the cornstarch. Shake well. If any lumps remain, skim them from the top of the mixture.
- Refrigerate the mixture until you are ready to use it. It keeps in the fridge for about two days.

Bruises

Create fake bruises by blending different colors of eye shadow.

Directions

- Apply a blot of deep blue powder eye shadow with a wet makeup brush. Use your fingertips to add blots of charcoal gray and blue shadows. Touch up the edges with a shimmery olive green. Smudge the bruise to complete.

Supplies

- ❑ deep blue powder eye shadow
- ❑ charcoal or smoke gray powder eye shadow
- ❑ shimmery green powder eye shadow
- ❑ makeup brush

Enjoy more spook-tacular fun in these collections from

GHOST HOUSE

CAMPFIRE GHOST STORIES

by Jo-Anne Christensen

Read-aloud stories perfect for the late evening hours around a campfire in the woods.

$10.95US/$14.95CDN • ISBN 1-894877-02-0
5.25" x 8.25" • 224 pages

HAUNTED HALLOWEEN STORIES

by Jo-Anne Christensen

Great read-aloud stories to send shivers down the spines of your audience! People of all ages will clamor to hear best-selling author Jo-Anne Christensen's latest contribution to Ghost House Books, this one a collection of fictional, dramatic tales involving Halloween. Take this book along to your next camping adventure and scare the wits out of your companions.

$10.95US/$14.95CDN • ISBN 1-894877-34-9
5.25" x 8.25" • 232 pages

PUMPKIN CARVING

The jack-o'-lantern is a central and traditional feature of Halloween. This book features tips and design templates that will make carving your pumpkins a snap.

$7.95US/$9.95CDN • ISBN 1-894877-26-8
8" x 10" • 48 pages

GHOSTS, WEREWOLVES, WITCHES AND VAMPIRES

by Jo-Anne Christensen

A collection of riveting short stories about four of the best-known creatures in paranormal mythology—witches, werewolves, vampires and ghosts. Although the accounts are dramatized, each is based on events believed to be true. Above all, they're fun to read, full of memorable characters.

$11.95US/$14.95CDN • ISBN 1-55105-333-0
5.25" x 8.25" • 224 pages

FIRESIDE GHOST STORIES

by A.S. Mott

Gather near a blazing fire and break out these spooky and heartwarming tales from author A.S. Mott. Get ready to pop the popcorn and snuggle under a blanket for *Fireside Ghost Stories*.

$10.95US/$14.95CDN • ISBN 1-894877-40-3
5.25" x 8.25" • 216 pages